Real-Life Drama for Real, Live Students

A Collection of Monologues,
Duet Acting Scenes,
and a
Full-Length Play

by Judy Truesdell Mecca

Incentive Publications, Inc.
Nashville, Tennessee

Illustrated by Gayle S. Harvey
Cover by Marta Drayton and Joe Shibley
Edited by Jan Keeling

ISBN 0-86530-352-5

PRINTED IN THE UNITED STATES OF AMERICA

Table of Contents

Preface

Real-Life Drama for Real, Live Students is a collection of scenes and short plays for young actors. Some are serious and deal with real-life problems and decisions that face our students. Some are funny, ranging from scenes that have quick wordplay and comic timing to scenes that present current issues using broad caricatures.

Who will use *Real-Life Drama?* Teachers of drama or speech classes! Any time a student is given a scene which delights him or her, touches off a creative spark, and provides lines which can be learned and delivered before the class, the student gains a little more self-confidence. Each time such a scene occurs, there is a little more communication between the student and the class, or between the student and the duet partner. There are roles in these plays which will seem like family members, friends . . . like the students themselves. There is a version of "Cinderella!" which would be a wonderful project for high school or middle school actors to present to younger students. Bus some young students to your school or go to them—and watch your own students turn into stars as they sign autographs for the younger students after the show.

Who else will use *Real-Life Drama*? Teachers of a non-drama subject, such as history, will find them useful. Your students can act out—or just read aloud—the historical scenes in this collection, such as the *real* story of Pocahontas and John Smith, presented with humorous banter that will amuse your class. The Watergate scandal is sorted through in one monologue. Your students can meet Susan B. Anthony. And there is a scene between Dr. and Mrs. Martin Luther King, Jr. These sketches offer a different way to present material that might seem a little dry coming straight out of a textbook.

Who else will find *Real-Life Drama* useful? Anyone concerned about the decisions and dangers that face our young people today, including P.E. and health teachers, counselors, English teachers . . . The scene "I'm Really Here" presents a young woman who feels as if she doesn't really exist unless she has "a boyfriend." In a frank monologue, she makes tough choices about what this means, and she changes the direction of her life by joining in a group activity. "The Dan and John Duet" presents two friends of different ethnic backgrounds who find that the differences in their backgrounds don't really matter. Your students need not learn lines and wear costumes to benefit from some of these scenes. Instead, you can make copies, read the scenes together, and discuss them as a class. Whether the scenes and plays are used in elaborate productions with costumes and props, or used to begin class discussions, your students will be sure to benefit from the communication of issues and ideas!

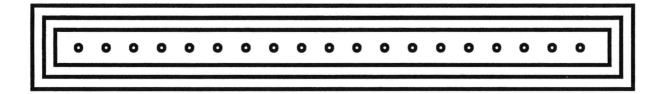

He Said, He Means

A Short Play for Two Girls and Two Boys

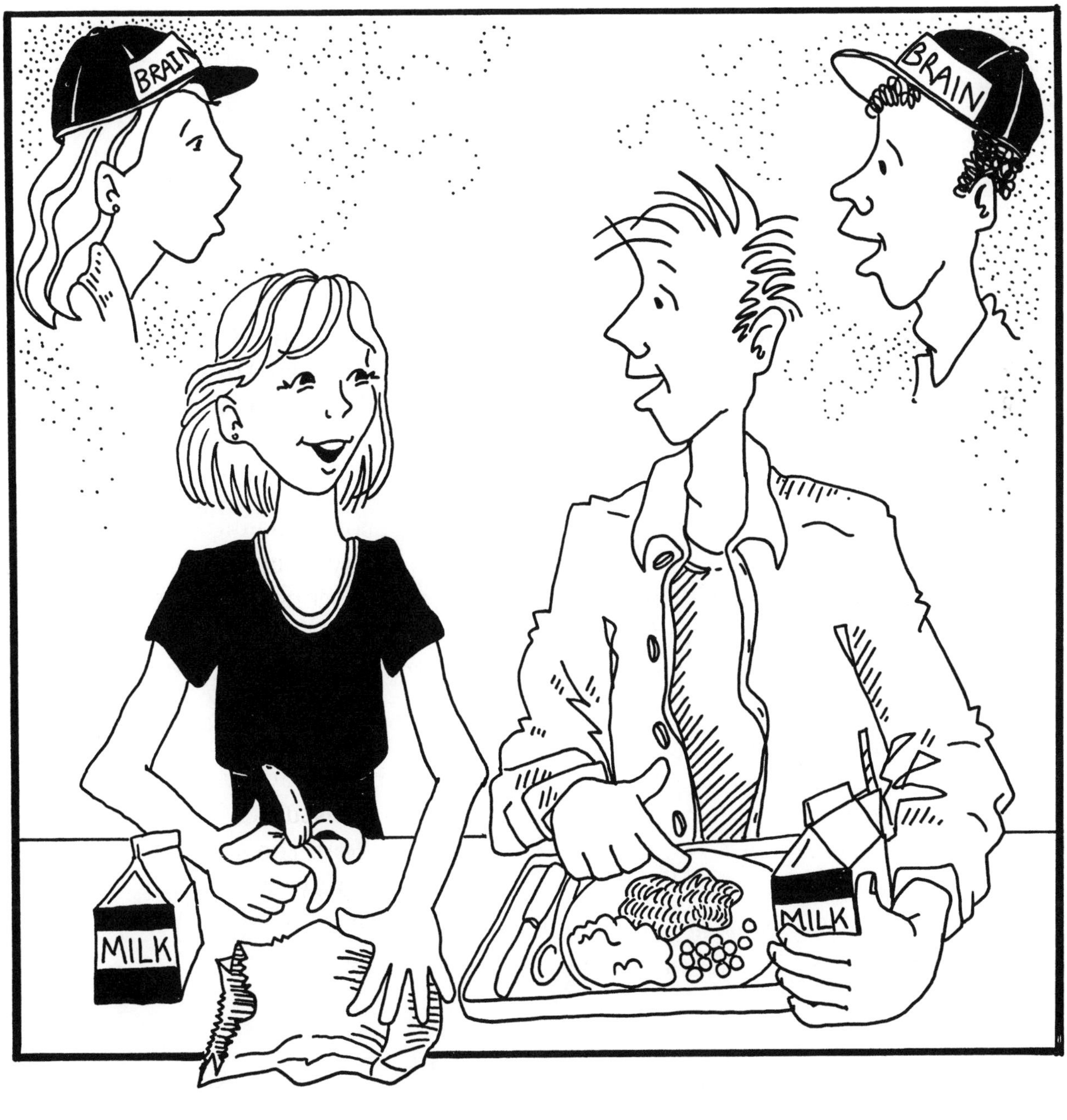

Exercises to Accompany He Said, He Means

1. This short play is about communication—or, more specifically, about thinking one thing but saying something else, often something entirely different. Think of a time when you misrepresented your feelings to someone—your parents, a friend, a teacher. How did it turn out? Were feelings hurt? Was tension created that might have been avoided? Or was someone actually spared who might have been hurt if your true feelings had been revealed? Discuss your thoughts as a class.

2. It's Amy's birthday. Her husband Andrew asks her what she wants for a gift. As they are having financial trouble, she says, "Oh, nothing." So that's what he gets her! What did she really mean? What should she have said? What does Andrew learn from this about his wife and about being married?

3. Pair off. Create a situation such as a first date, a brother and sister sharing the television, or two friends at a game or shopping together. Invent a problem for the two to solve. (Does one want to go to the movies but the other can't afford it? Is one friend jealous of how cute the other looks in her new outfit?) Improvise a scene. The first time, have the two characters deceive each other. Under no circumstances should you have them reveal their true feelings. See where this leads. Then, using the same characters in the same situation with the same conflict, improvise truthful dialogue—let them say what they really feel and see where this leads.

4. Lots of communication between humans takes place without any spoken words at all, but instead through facial expressions, hand gestures, body language. Have someone go before the class and make an announcement. ("I got an after-school job!" or "We're getting married," or "I've decided to join the Marines," etc.) Then, one by one, have each member of the class demonstrate his or her response to this news without saying a word, just by physical expression. You may wish to be someone other than yourself. For instance, if a student announces, "I'm running for president!" be his wife and react to the news. See how much communication is possible without saying a word!

5. For the next few days, keep a journal of instances of communication you observe between people. Notice friends who are being very truthful with each other, and notice people who are deceiving each other for some reason (like the girl who doesn't do her homework and tries to convince the teacher it really wasn't her fault, or your brothers and sisters as they talk to your parents). Decide whether you think we are truthful most of the time—or not.

Cast

(in order of appearance)

Tony	Jenna's Brain
Jenna	Tony's Brain

He Said, He Means

A Short Play for Two Girls and Two Boys

(Tony and Jenna meet in the lunchroom. Tony has a cafeteria tray; Jenna has a sack lunch.)

Tony: Hey, Jenna.

Jenna: Hey, Tony.

Tony *(sitting down)*: How did you do on your math test?

Jenna *(joining him)*: I think I did okay.

(Enter Jenna's Brain.)

Jenna's Brain: Hi, I'm Jenna's Brain. I know, you were expecting me to be a little bit more gray and wrinkled. Sorry to disappoint you. I'm not the actual brain sitting in her head protected by her skull; I'm the part that thinks one thing while she says another. Like this. Watch.

Jenna: Yeah, the test was pretty hard, but I think I aced it.

Jenna's Brain: What she means is . . . "I know you're really smart in math, Tony, and I want to impress you."

Tony: It was really tough, that's true.

(Enter Tony's Brain.)

Tony's Brain: Thank you, thank you, it's me, Tony's Brain. At least what's left of Tony's brain. If he doesn't start wearing a helmet when he skates . . . anyway, allow me to interpret . . .

Tony: It was really hard—I hope I passed.

Tony's Brain: Tony knows good and well he passed with flying colors. He means, "I know I passed with flying colors, Jenna, but I like you and I don't want you to think I'm a geek."

Jenna's Brain: A geek?

Tony's Brain: You know, like a schoolboy. An egghead.

Jenna's Brain: She doesn't think that! She likes him!

Tony's Brain: I know that and you know that, but . . .

Jenna *(looking at TONY's lunch)*: What's that meat there? Looks kinda scary.

Jenna's Brain: Jenna's self-conscious because she brought a sack lunch instead of buying. She doesn't want Tony to think she's poor.

Tony: Some kind of mystery meat, I don't know. I think it might be "filet of the new assistant principal."

(Jenna laughs.)

Tony's Brain: Excuse me? Are we trying to be funny here?

Jenna's Brain: Trying is right . . . But it's okay. Jenna thinks that . . .

Jenna: You're really funny, Tony.

Jenna's Brain: Jenna thinks, "I did think that was really funny, but why did I give him a compliment like that! He'll think I'm flirting with him for sure."

Tony's Brain: Well, isn't she? I mean, mildly?

Jenna's Brain: Well, yes! But she can't be so bold! What if he gets up and runs off?

Tony: Your mom make your lunch?

Jenna's Brain: Oh, oh! Here's trouble!

Tony's Brain: Look—Tony's mother works two jobs and doesn't have a lot of time for him. She's way too busy to fix him a lunch—she's doing good to remember she has a son who needs lunch money handed to him. He really means, "How cool, your mother loves you enough to slap some peanut butter on some bread."

Jenna's Brain: That's not what she'll think, though. She'll think that Tony thinks she's a baby.

Jenna: Yeah. I guess she still thinks I'm in elementary school.

Jenna's Brain: Told ya.

Tony: Remember those lunch boxes we used to carry?

Jenna: With superheroes and fashion dolls?

Tony's Brain: Oh, oh! Real connection! Being frank with each other! Communication!

Jenna's Brain: Will you shut up and listen?

Tony: Superheroes and fashion dolls? On the same lunch box? That I'd like to see!

Tony's Brain: Oh no, he crashes and burns with another poor attempt at humor! He's still trying to impress her with his wit.

Jenna's Brain: Don't forget, she really does think he's clever. Though I wish someone would tell me why.

Jenna: Tony, I was thinking . . .

Jenna's Brain: She's really nervous! She likes this guy and respects him because he's smart and nice.

Jenna: My mom's got some sort of PTA thing at the house after school . . .

Tony's Brain: Ow! There's that "caring mom" thing again! Tony's really jealous.

Jenna: So I was wondering . . .

Tony's Brain: Oh, now he's really interested! Is he about to hear something "after school-ish"?

Jenna: I was wondering if you'd like to go to the mall for a little while?

Jenna's Brain: That was exactly what she was thinking! You go, girl!

Tony: I'd really like that, Jenna!

Tony's Brain: And that's what he was really thinking! Oh no, we're about to be out of a job! *(acting like the witch in* The Wizard of Oz) I'm melting! I'm melting! What a world!

Jenna's Brain: Shhhh!

Jenna: Great! Let's meet near the gym after the last bell, okay?

Tony: Sounds good. Oh, wait . . .

Tony's Brain: Oops, he's in trouble now. He told his buddy he'd meet him after school.

Tony: I told this guy named Connor I'd meet him then. He's got some sort of a problem he wants to talk to me about.

Jenna's Brain: Oh, great. Now she'll think he's giving her the brushoff.

Jenna: Okay, forget it. Some other time.

Tony's Brain: Come on, Tony! Work this out! He really likes Jenna. He'll work this out.

Tony: Wait, I know. I'll talk to him in History this afternoon and tell him to call me tonight.

Jenna's Brain: Okay, that'll work, but is it too late? Does she have enough self-esteem to believe him and keep the plans?

Tony: So, do you still want to meet?

Jenna: Well . . .

Jenna's Brain: Come on, girl, take a chance! He's a stand-up guy. It's good that he's honorable where his friends are concerned too!

Tony's Brain *(sarcastically)*: Oh, please . . .

Jenna: Yeah, Tony, that sounds great!

Jenna's Brain: She means it!

Tony: Great! I'm looking forward to it.

Tony's Brain: He means it!

Jenna: Bye, Tony. I'll see you after school.

Tony: I'll be there.

(Tony and Jenna exit.)

Jenna's Brain: Ah, a happy ending. They couldn't have done it without us.

Tony's Brain: I don't know. Lately he's been getting pretty good at saying what he means.

Jenna's Brain: He'll never have a career in politics if he keeps that up.

Tony's Brain: No joke.

Jenna's Brain: See you at the mall?

Tony's Brain: Let's shop till they drop!

(They link arms and exit.)

Does This Seem Fair?

A Historical Monologue for a Girl

Exercises to Accompany Does This Seem Fair?

1. Susan B. Anthony's historic voter registration took place in 1872. Subtract that year from the current year and see how relatively recent an event this was. How have things changed for women since that time? List some opportunities women now have that were never considered in 1872. Project the same number of years into the future and imagine the changes that may take place by then.
2. Many of us imagine ourselves to be very open-minded now. But are there still some groups who are prevented from being a part of their country the way they would like?
3. Write a brief monologue in which you portray one of the barbers on hand when Susan B. Anthony comes in and demands to vote. Are you critical of her? Do you think she's overstepped her bounds? Are you somewhat in awe of her, and do you respect her courage? Use your **Creating Believable Characters** worksheet on page 111 to help make your character three-dimensional and real.
4. Just for fun, write a song as if you were Susan B. Anthony. Will it be country-western? A blues song? A rap?

Does This Seem Fair?

A Historical Monologue for a Girl

(The scene begins with Susan B. Anthony seated at a desk. She is opening a letter. Several letters are already open on her desk, and we see that many contain money. There are books and newspapers on her desk as well.)

Susan: It is the late 1800s. Does a woman in the United States of America have the right to cast a vote for the candidate of her choice?

She does not.

If a woman and man should divorce, who has the right to the children?

The man.

If a woman works, sometimes for as little as 37 cents for a 14-hour day, may her husband collect her salary?

Yes, he may.

If a woman has an inheritance from her parents, may her husband take it from her at will?

Yes, he may, and with the blessing of the court of the United States of America.

Does this seem fair? To me, Susan B. Anthony, it does not. No, indeed.

(rising)

Why on earth should the women of the United States of America not enjoy the same rights as the men of the same fine country? Black men across America are now considered citizens. They can now vote. Is a woman, whatever her color, somehow less a citizen than any man?

The Fourteenth Amendment to the Constitution of the United States of America states *(consulting a book)* that "a person born or naturalized in the United States is a citizen, a citizen has a right to vote." Did you hear me mention the gender of that person? Did you hear me even use the word "man"?

No, indeed.

That is why I marched into the barbershop of the eighth precinct in Rochester, New York, where men were registering voters. I announced that I was there to register to vote. "You don't want to vote, Miss Anthony," one of them said to me, doing everything except patting me on the head. "This is man's business! Go on home and put your thoughts on more suitable subjects."

Like doilies or toilet water, I suppose.

I read the Fourteenth Amendment to him. I asked him to show me where it excused women from the responsibility to vote. He could not. He could scarcely close his mouth. I feared a fly would fly in, like the climate there, and set up housekeeping in the barber's open mouth!

I registered to vote that day.

What followed was interesting, exciting, and ridiculous. All of Rochester heard of this event and soon all of the newspapers in the country were telling the story of this *(chuckling)* hardheaded woman who invaded the barbershop and demanded a ballot. The trouble really began when I actually cast my ballot for a representative of the Congress of the United States in the general elections on November 5, 1872. Fairly soon after that, I was apprehended and placed under arrest! I was charged with "illegal voting." When I appeared before the district attorney, I requested that he schedule my trial for after December 10. I had public speaking dates up until that date, and I didn't mean to break my word.

He blustered. He reminded me that I was under arrest, after all, and what business did I have requesting when my trial would be? He sputtered. He grew red in the face.

He scheduled my trial for after the tenth of December.

And at all my speaking engagements, I asked of my audiences, "Is it a crime for a citizen of the United States to vote?" I ask you today, "Is it a crime for a citizen of the United States to vote?"

(waits for audience to respond)

I see we agree.

When I was finally tried for the heinous crime of illegally voting, my attorneys argued that my only crime was my sex. They argued that women had no recourse, no way to bring suit against an abusive husband, or to regain something legally hers. A woman could be taxed, but could not choose who should represent her in government. Indeed, there were not even any women lawyers to represent me!

He made a terrific argument. Couldn't have put it better myself.

But the Honorable Judge Hunt ruled against me. He ordered the jury to bring in a verdict of guilty!

I was charged to pay five hundred dollars, which I refused to pay. I said that I would never pay a penny of an unjust penalty! And I left the courthouse.

(chuckling)

I think Judge Hunt wishes he had made a different decision that day. I have opened letter after letter from man and woman alike, wishing me well, sending me money, and admonishing the judge. *(picking up a newspaper)* Many of the nation's newspapers have taken my side and some have even called for the judge's impeachment. One newspaper says *(reading)*, "It is not only Susan Anthony he has insulted, but he has insulted all American womanhood."

Truly, he did insult all womanhood—and all manhood as well. If we continue to choose certain groups of people to limit this way, to limit how they may contribute—doesn't this insult us all? Man and woman alike?

Does this seem fair?

I think we're on our way, now. I think a great eye has blinked open across the country and, before long, women will not only be allowed to vote, but to attend the finest colleges in the land. We'll contribute in the world of business, and stand shoulder to shoulder with our brothers. Not ahead of them, pushing them back—but together, hand in hand, arm in arm.

Does this seem fair? It does to me. What's your vote?

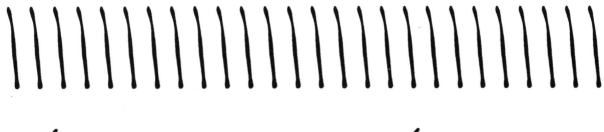

Cut To The Clique

A "Game Show" Short Play

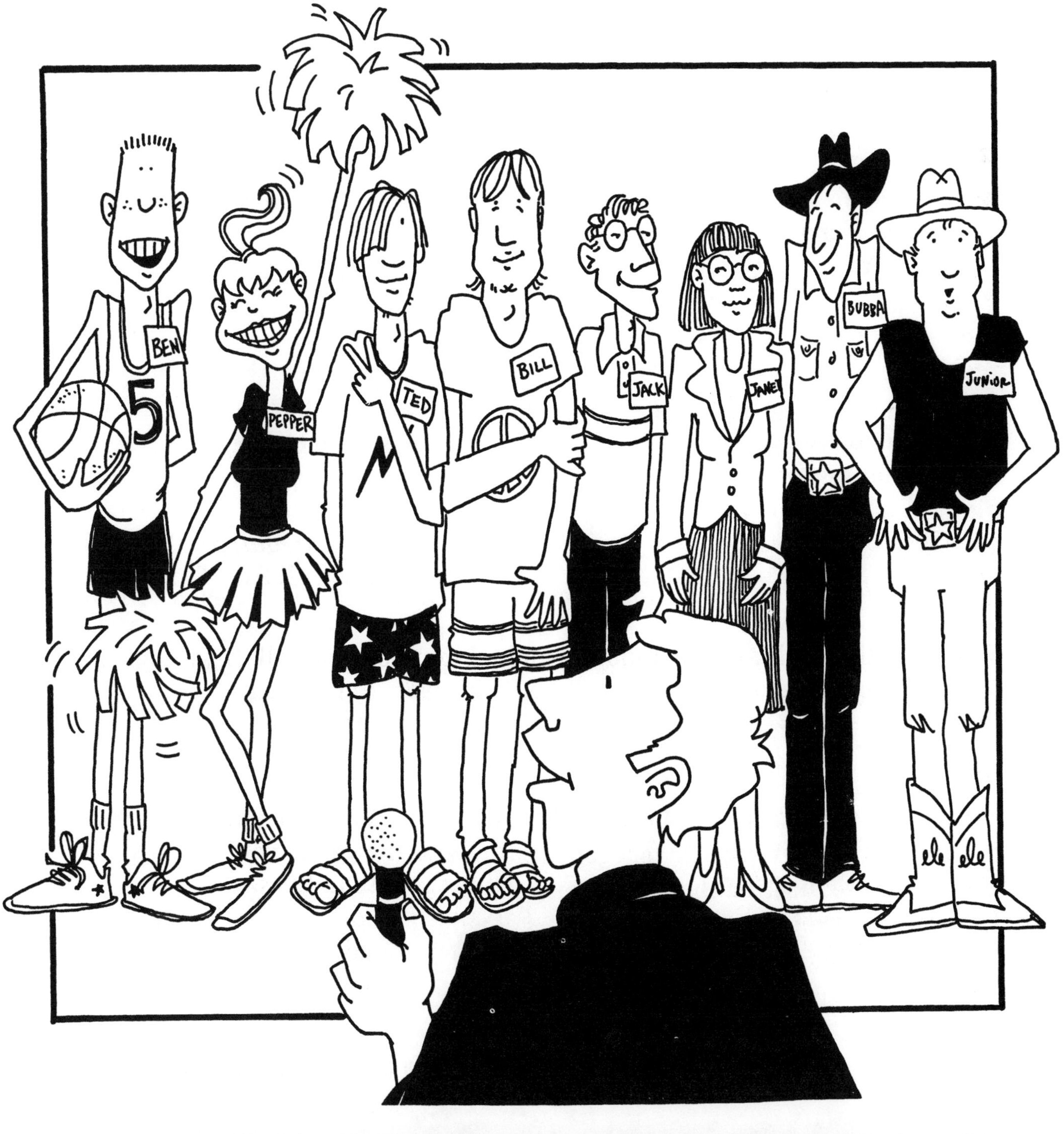

About *Cut To The Clique*

In many schools, students seem to group themselves together in "cliques." A **clique** is defined in the dictionary as an "exclusive group of people." Somehow the people who love sports seem to find themselves together in the lunchroom, and those to whom it is important to dress in the latest style from the latest store in the latest mall seem to group together . . . and on and on.

You may or may not have cliques in your school, or if you do, you may very well call them by another name. This short play, *Cut to the Clique,* features a game-show style competition among four cliques at Millhouse Middle School: **The Jocks,** who are sports boys and girls; **The Headbangers,** who enjoy hard rock music and sport long hair; **The School Boys and Girls,** who try (way too hard) to do their best in their school work; and finally, **The Ropers,** whose hobbies include agriculture and rodeo. (If you live in the north or eastern part of the country, you may not know about Ropers . . . just think "yee haw" and you'll get the idea.) This play is set at Millhouse Middle School, which is completely fictitious. These cliques are portrayed in what is called a stereotypical manner—that is, the traits and characteristics which a particular group might have are exaggerated for comic value. For instance, Pepper Spirit, the cheerleader, is snobby and bored and only interested in the tanning salon and the mall. This is a stereotypical view of cheerleaders. In real life, some wonderful girls cheer their schools on to victory—and may volunteer at the local hospital after school, or may contribute part of their allowance to the support of an orphan. The point is, Pepper is a stereotypical cheerleader for the sake of humor, and so are the other student characters.

Maybe you do have cliques at your school, such as "Nerds," "Preps," "Skateboarders," or "Duds." It might be fun to substitute one of the actual groups at your school for one of the cliques in *Cut to the Clique,* especially to replace one of the groups in the play which may not be familiar to you. You'll have to write new dialogue that would be appropriate to this group. (See **Creating Believable Characters** worksheet on page 111 for some help.)

Maybe you would rather set the play at your school instead of Millhouse. Whichever way you choose to go, keep in mind that the point of doing this piece is not to mock groups or insult those who think and dress differently than you. Rather, it is to have a good time, enjoy some laughs, and perhaps come to the realization that the whole "clique" and "group" thing is pretty silly. Perhaps you might think in terms of what you have in common with your fellow students—rather than in terms of your differences.

Exercises to Accompany Cut To The Clique

1. Are similarities often more important than differences? Try this exercise. Take one character from each clique in the play and improvise a scene in which they must all work together toward a goal. Do they decorate for the Halloween party? Do they plan a fund-raiser for a class trip? How do they interact with each other? Are they able to successfully rise above their differences and find common ground?

2. For class discussion: Do cliques make students feel good, as if they are part of a group and have acceptance? Or do they make them feel bad, as if they are being excluded? Do cliques emphasize the things we have in common or the ways in which we feel different?

3. Design a "costume plot" for this play. That is, do a sketch of each character and decide what he or she will wear. You may wish to take photographs, for instance, of cheerleaders or football players whom you know for the "Jocks," or work purely from imagination. Visit the local fabric store and ask them for material swatches if you like. Be very specific about colors and the overall look of each character's costume. (Doing this exercise doesn't mean you'll actually make or gather these costumes—but approach it as if you had an unlimited budget. What would your dream costumes look like?)

4. Choose a character from this play and write a brief monologue for him or her. Think in terms of giving more depth to the character than is shown in this play. Look past the stereotype, think about creating a more "real" person out of one of these students. What would he or she want to talk about? Try thinking creatively rather than looking toward the obvious. Don't have Ted or Bill talking about the history of rock music—have one of them talking about his childhood, maybe a particularly touching memory about his grandfather. Or put Janet in a situation in which she didn't excel and couldn't no matter how hard she tried.

Cast

(in order of appearance)

MC

Ben Gaylord of the "Jocks"

Pepper Spirit of the "Jocks"

Ted of the "Headbangers"

Bill of the "Headbangers"

Jack of the "School Boys and Girls"

Janet of the "School Boys and Girls"

Bubba Junior of the "Ropers"

Junior Junior of the "Ropers"

Mike, the announcer

Cut To The Clique

A "Game Show" Short Play

(This is a game show in which four of the little groups or "cliques" at Millhouse Middle School participate. As the scene begins, we see the Jocks, the Ropers, the School Boys and Girls, and the Headbangers assembled, ready to play.)

MC: Hello, ladies and gentlemen, and welcome to **Cut to the Clique,** the game show that pits clique against clique as the clock tick tock ticks—in an effort to find out who really reigns supreme at Millhouse Middle School! Let's meet our contestants. *(moving to the Jocks)* First, for the Jocks. He's quarterback of the football team in the fall, star forward for the basketball team in the winter, captain of the baseball team in the spring, and in the off season—wait, there is no off season for this guy!

Ben Gaylord: Yes there is! For one week in July, I work at "Sports Am My Life" Sporting Goods Store!

MC: What a sport! Help me please to welcome number 12, number 34, and number 50, Ben Gaylord!

(As MC says number 12, Ben stands and strikes a football pose; number 34, he pretends to be at bat; number 50, he pantomimes shooting a basket. Upon hearing his name, he cheers for himself, arms high over his head.)

Pepper: Ben, please, you're sprinkling me!

Ben: Sorry, Pepper. *(sits, looking crestfallen)*

MC: Moving on to Ben's teammate, head cheerleader, founder of the Millhouse Middle School Pep Squad, and holder of the school record for the most butcher paper painted, meet Miss Pepper Spirit!

(Pepper gets up, completely bored until she takes center stage and begins to cheer. Suddenly she comes alive like a toy whose batteries have just been plugged in.)

Pepper: Ready, okay!
The Jocks, you know, for sure, we rule!
Our players are the coolest cool!

We lead the way for the whole school—

You're not a Jock, you are a pitiful loser with no redeeming social value!

Ben: Gya, Pepper, that didn't even rhyme.

Pepper: Well, I had to write it in a really big hurry, okay? And my nails were wet.

(She sits.)

MC: Thank you Pepper Spirit! And by the way, which do you have the most of? Pep or Spirit?

Pepper: Excuse me?

MC: Never mind! Let's move on to our next competitors, Team Headbangers! First, Bill! *(He turns his index card over and over.)* Bill, don't you have a last name?

Bill: What?

MC: I say, don't you have a last name?

Bill: I used to, Dude, but I think I lost it somewhere.

Ted: All right! He lost it somewhere!

MC: And this is Ted! Ted, I'm not showing a last name here for you either!

Ted *(pause, then . . .)*: What?

MC: I say, I . . . oh never mind, let's wish Bill and Ted good luck in their excellent adventure today.

(Bill and Ted pantomime playing guitars and make hard rock guitar noises.)

MC: Moving right along, let's visit our next team, the School Boys and Girls!

Jack: We're so excited to be here, aren't we, Janet?

Janet: That's ever so right, Jack. We're happy to represent Millhouse Middle School in any forum, but especially one in which we can engage in friendly competition with our fellow classmates, the Headbangers, Jocks, and Ropers!

Jack: Because after all, we're one big happy family, aren't we, Janet? The student body of Millhouse Middle School!

Janet: That's super right, Jack! And here's hoping our competition will be friendly, beneficial to us all, and most important, a learning and growing experience! Right, Headbangers? Jocks? Ropers?

(The other teams have gradually stopped fidgeting and talking among themselves and have started to stare at the School Boys and Girls with their mouths hanging open.)

Jack: Right, fellow classmates?

Janet: I guess they're a little nervous in advance of the competition. Don't worry, though, competitors! Jack and I have spent six hours every night at the library after we've finished our chores at our respective homes, and we've compiled some data of which you may all avail yourselves! Here! *(She produces a long computer printout which unscrolls and falls to the floor.)* Surely the answer to any question is here.

Jack *(inhaling deeply)*: Nothing like the smell of raw data, eh, Janet?

Janet: I'm getting butterflies in my stomach, just looking at it. And speaking of butterflies, everyone, did you know that the most common species of butterfly in the United States is the monarch?

Jack: Yes I did! Its average wing span is 8 centimeters . . .

Janet: And it generally feeds on mulberry leaves and the sugar from discarded frozen juice bar wrappers!

Pepper *(to MC)*: Somebody stop them before they hurt themselves.

MC: Moving on . . . really quickly . . . to our fourth and final team, please give a warm welcome to the Ropers!

Bubba Junior: Hello, Mr. MC, my name is Bubba Junior, I was named after my daddy Bubba who was somebody's brother. And this here is my teammate and fellow member of the Future Farmers of the Future, Junior Junior.

Junior Junior: Howdy there, Mr. MC, Junior Junior Turnipseed here. I was named after my father who was . . .

MC: Don't tell me, let me guess. Somebody's son.

Junior Junior: Well, I reckon he was somebody's son, Mr. MC, I mean aren't we all? But naw, what I was fixin' to say was he was a rodeo rider for years, then he raised hogs for the county fair, and now he's a high school principal.

MC: And so you're named Junior Junior.

Junior Junior: What?

Bill: That's what I say, dude . . . what?

MC: Moving right along! We'll be asking questions on a wide variety of topics today. The first person to hit his or her buzzer will be given a chance to answer, and the team with the most correct answers will win prizes selected especially for them! Tell them what they'll win, Don Pardo!

Mike *(offstage with a microphone)*: Um . . . there's not anybody here named Don Pardo—my name is MIKE and I'm supposed to read this list of prizes.

MC *(sighing)*: Some days it doesn't pay to get out of bed.

Mike: Should I go ahead and read this list?

MC: Yes, please.

Mike: Okay. Today's winning team will receive 25 pounds of fertilizer from Pewey's Feed and Seed Store. Your neighbors will always know you're coming when you fertilize with Pewey's.

Junior Junior: Yee haw!

Bubba Junior: We could sure shovel some of that there!

Mike: I'm glad you're excited about the prizes, Junior Junior and Bubba Junior, but could you hold it down? We want to finish sometime today.

Bubba Junior: I'm sorry. I guess I thought you were prerecorded.

Mike: Even if I were, we still need to get through this list. Our winners will also receive an afternoon of luxury at Hang Ten Nail and Tanning Salon . . .

Pepper: Now that's worth leaving the house for.

Mike: . . . and your weight in liniment from The Sports Injury House.

Ben: Been there, done that!

Mike: Lucky winning competitors will also receive a complete set of encyclopedias . . .

Jack: What're "encyclopedias"?

Janet: I think they're like a prehistoric Internet. You know, like real books.

Jack: Like with pages?

Janet: I think.

Mike: And last but not least . . . or maybe it is . . . Pink Floyd's Christmas Album, "Hang Your Stockings on the Wall."

Bill: Dude!

Ted: Vintage!

Bill: What's an album?

Ted: It's like a smushed-out CD.

Mike: And everyone who plays today will receive a $25 gift certificate from the Fleegel catalogue. That's the Fleegel catalogue, Chicago, Illinois. Back to you, MC! I never caught your real name, sorry . . .

MC: Thank you Don Pardo, or whomever you are . . .

Janet: That's whoever!

Jack: Nominative case!

MC: Well, whatever the case, here's our first question. Contestants, ready? Name a verb that means to handle roughly, such as what a grizzly bear might do to an unsuspecting camper. *(Janet rings in.)* Janet for the School Boys and Girls?

Janet: Maim? Bruise? Annihilate?

MC: Just one guess, please! But no, sorry, those are incorrect . . .

Bubba Junior: Hog tie?

Pepper: Oh, I'm so sure "hog tie" is the correct answer. As if.

Ben: Pound? Pummel? Trounce? Sack? Drop for a loss?

MC: Contestants, please remember to ring in!

Ben *(ringing in)*: Pound? Pummel?

Jack: I'm sure that's wrong, but what nice alliteration!

Janet: Yes, but now he'll say "trounce" and ruin it.

Ben: Trounce?

Bill: What?

MC: Sorry, I haven't yet heard the correct answer to "name a verb that means to handle roughly, such as what a grizzly bear might do to an unsuspecting camper."

Pepper: Oh, please, you bunch of lame-o's, it's MAUL.

MC: That's right, Pepper! A point for the Jocks.

Ben: How did you know that, Pepper?

Pepper: Did you ever meet a cheerleader who didn't know about the mall? On with the game!

MC: Next question: Name something ever served in the Millhouse Middle School cafeteria that tasted good!

(Silence, as all think.)

MC: Okay, toss that one out. Next question. Please translate this sentence into understandable English: "I was fixin' to pitch a hissy fit when my dad tumped over the bucket and spilt all the minners into the floor of the double wide."

Ted: What?

Junior Junior: Aw shucks, Mr. MC, that's simple. He was right upset when his dad accidentally knocked the bait bucket over and all the live bait escaped onto the floor of the mobile home.

Bubba Junior: But he didn't throw a fuss quite yet—he was just thinking about it. He was fixin' to.

Pepper *(sarcastically)*: Yee haw.

MC: Yee haw indeed, and a point for the Ropers!

Jack: FYI, speaking of "minnows," *The Minnow* was the name of the boat which wrecked and was marooned on a desert island in the popular situation comedy *Gilligan's Island.*

Janet: Right, Jack. That same popular sit-com is shown in syndication now on seventeen different stations around the world!

Jack: And P.S.—Jerry Lewis is the most popular American comic in France!

Ted: What?

MC: Fascinating, but let's move on to our next question. Astronomers estimate that if it were possible to stack all the moons of all the planets one on top of another, it would create a stack of moons exactly the same depth as the circumference of what planet?

Jack and Janet *(hugging and screaming excitedly)*: Mercury!

Jack: That was hardly fair though, Mr. MC.

Janet: That was our Science Fair Project last year!

MC: Nonetheless, a point goes to the School Boys and Girls!

Jack and Janet: Rah, rah, sis boom bah

Yeaaaaaa homework!

Pepper: Hey . . . you don't try to lead cheers, I won't try to learn anything in school. Deal?

MC: Now for our final question. Ready? Give an example of an interrogative word that is neither "why," "when," nor "who."

Bill: What?

MC: That's right! All four teams now have a point—and we're out of time! Looks as if we have a four-way tie today—proving once and for all that all cliques are created equal! Thanks and goodnight!

(All blow kisses and wave good-bye.)

WHATTA PLAN

A Rap Song

WHATTA PLAN

A Rap Song to the "Tune" of ***Whatta Man*** *by Salt-N-Pepa*

I want to talk to you now about my plans for the future.
I'm gonna make my own way, never be a moocher.
Graduate from school, get myself an honest job
And never be tempted to steal, cheat, or rob.

I'll be true to my word, honest as can be.
My friends will know they can all count on me.
You'll be proud to be my friend, never disgraced.
If I say I'll be there, you better save me a place.

I have only one body for my time on this earth
So I will take care of it for all that it is worth.
Health and fitness is the way I'm gonna go
So if you say "drugs," I will just say "no."

Whatta plan, whatta plan, whatta plan, whatta mighty good plan.
It's a "lookin' to the future" plan.
Whatta plan, whatta plan, whatta plan, whatta mighty nice plan.
It's a "workin' my way up" plan.

I want to be a teacher and help a kid like me
Who can be anything that he wants to be.
At the end of the day I'll give 'em "high five."
May not make a lot of money, but I'll touch a lot of lives.

Professional sports is the way I want to go
So I'm building up my body from my head down to my toe.
I will practice after school, I'll always see action
And I will play in two sports as if I were Bo Jackson.

Gonna work with computers to keep myself alive—
Boot myself up, I have a real hard drive.
Or maybe I'll have kids and have an office in my house
And I will teach my babies how to double click a mouse.

Whatta plan, whatta plan, whatta plan, whatta solid good plan.
It's a "watch me, here I go" plan
Whatta plan, whatta plan, whatta plan, whatta mighty fair plan.
It's a "takin' care of bizness" plan.

When I think of the future, this should be apparent—
The most important job is to be a good parent.
I'll raise my children to respect any race.
They will make this country and this world a better place.

I want to be a scientist who finds the answer
To why we have diseases like AIDS and cancer.
I want to give families a reason to hope.
I'll spend my days looking down a microscope.

I want a job that will make a real difference
And prove for all time that a girl can go the distance.
So follow my career and wonder where I went.
Wo! I'm at the White House! I'm a woman president!

Whatta plan, whatta plan, whatta plan, whatta mighty swell plan.
It's a "get on up and go" plan.
Whatta plan, whatta plan, whatta plan, whatta mighty righteous plan
It's the "opposite of lazy" plan.
Whatta plan, whatta plan, whatta plan, whatta mighty sound plan
It's an "I can really do it" plan.
Whatta plan, whatta plan, whatta plan, whatta mighty strong plan.
It's a "nothin's gonna stop me" plan!

WE'RE GOIN' FOR IT!

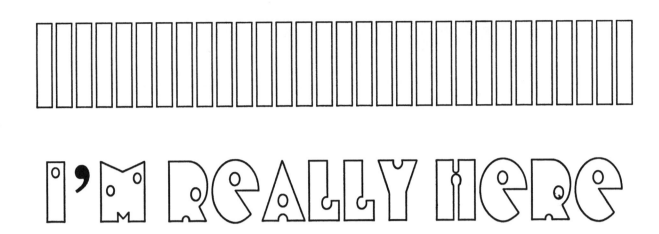

I'M REALLY HERE

A Dramatic Monologue for a Girl

Exercises to Accompany I'M REALLY HERE

1. What do you think about this monologue? Do you think there really are young people who only feel "real" when involved with an opposite-sex person? Have you ever felt this way? How might these feelings get in the way of your success? How might they be physically dangerous? It would be great if your class members feel comfortable enough with each other to discuss this as a class.
2. The girl in the monologue feels that her worth is defined through her relationships with boys. Do you think *girls* are more likely to feel this way than *boys*? Discuss this as a class.
3. Think about the girl in the monologue. How might her life be different five years in the future if she had not joined the volleyball team? Write a brief paper, diary entry, or short monologue as the character at nineteen years of age.
4. Noted psychotherapist Dr. Laura C. Schlessinger has written a book called *Ten Stupid Things Women Do To Mess Up Their Lives* which is published by Villard Books, a division of Random House, Inc., 201 East 50th Street, New York, NY 10022. If you would like to read more about this type of behavior, this book is a terrific source. Please ask a parent or teacher to look it over to make sure the language and subject matter contained in the book is suitable for your use.

I'M REALLY HERE

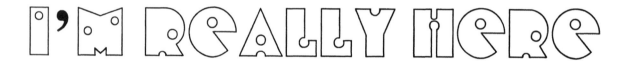

A Dramatic Monologue for a Girl

This may sound like a stupid question, but can you really see me? Am I really here?

I don't know who to blame for this—maybe my parents, somehow. Let me tell you. I am sixteen years old and I don't have any idea of who I am—or if I'm really even here—except when I have a boyfriend.

I know that sounds crazy. Of course I know who I am, I know my name and my address and where I go to school, and all that is a part of what makes me who I am. But I really don't feel THERE or like I really exist unless I have a serious relationship in my life. A serious male/female, boyfriend/girlfriend, "I'll-call-you-when-I-get-home-from-football-practice" type relationship.

I started feeling this way pretty young. I mean, I didn't think I was young then, but now I do, when I look back. It was the summer after the fifth grade and I was home with nothing to do. Both my parents were working, and since I'm the oldest, I had to stay home with my little brother and sister. So I was out on the curb in front of my house. I know, you want to make some joke about putting out the trash—well, don't, okay? Anyway, I was just sitting on the curb when this guy came by. Walked by. Named Jimmy. He lived on the next street over and he was walking up to the recreation center. I said "hi" and he said "hi" and he asked me my name and I told him and I asked him for a drink of his soda and he said "okay" and he sat down for a few minutes. Well, after a while he had to go, but I asked him if he'd stop back by on his way home and he said he would. So I went back inside the house and sat by the window and when I saw him coming down the street, I went out as if I were going to the mailbox. Then I pretended that I had just come out for the mail and what a coincidence that he was coming back down my street! He stopped again and now it was getting kind of dark, and so when he left I asked him if he would like to kiss me and he did. And I liked it a lot. I mean—I liked the kissing pretty well, but what I mostly liked was this: for that minute, while he was standing there holding his basketball on his hip, I was the most important thing in his world. He wasn't thinking about anything else but me and that made me feel very special. It made me feel I was real. As if I were actually THERE.

Jimmy and I kept meeting and kissing for the rest of the summer, but when school started I didn't see him any more. He was a few years older and went to another school. I was a little bit sad and missed him some, but mostly I felt I just . . . disappeared for a while. Until I met this guy named Jason at school who said he thought I was kind of cute and so I agreed to meet him after school to talk about that a little more. We met and talked and did some kissing and Jason liked me so much that he gave me an ID bracelet to wear. Now I really felt . . . definite. As if I were outlined in with a big black felt-tip marker or something. We said we were "going out." He came over and we walked up to the rec center and we kissed a lot behind my next-door neighbor's car. And I started to feel I needed to be with Jason all the time. Like I would wait outside in the mornings so that I could walk to school with him. And I would hang around the lunchroom and wait for him so we could eat lunch together. Sometimes that made him unhappy because he wanted to eat with his friends, you know, guys. But I didn't care because even if he was mad at me, I was someone real enough to be mad at. Does that make sense? I was important enough to be Jason's girlfriend who had made him mad. But I kept waiting for him and calling him on the phone and stuff and finally he didn't come by my house on the way to school. I thought he was staying home, maybe sick, but when I called his house, they told me he was fine. I guess he walked a different way to school. And when I saw him at lunch, he looked the other way and got into a real serious conversation with somebody else. It made me want to disappear—what am I saying? It made me feel as if I had disappeared.

This went on and on and on. There was Joel, who used to play touch football in the street with my neighbor's little boy, and there was Mike who lived across the alley, and another guy who was also named Mike who was older than me, a lot older, and worked at the Quick Mart down the street. I really liked the idea of someone older with an actual job thinking about me and making plans that had me in them, but then he wanted to do more things together than just kissing, if you know what I mean. I had to think about that for a while. I won't say I wasn't tempted. I mean, how much more important could a girl feel than that? But finally I decided not to, mostly because of being scared of AIDS. I had thought for a while that there was no way I could get AIDS since I'm not a man. And a particular kind of man, you know. But then I saw a film at school that let me know that no one is excused or protected, no one at all. At least not yet. So I decided to tell Mike "no." And that was very, very hard because he went away then. And left me—you know. Not there anymore.

But lately I've gotten into something that has made me feel a little different and I want this to work but I'm really scared. This may sound nuts, but I tried out for this volleyball team at the rec center. I don't know why I did it except that I wanted a little exercise so I could continue to eat everything I want and not grow out of my jeans, you know? And they play on Saturday afternoons, not a time when too much else is going on. Well, there are a couple of guys on the team, but there are all these really fun girls, too. And it turns out I'm a good volleyball player! Who would've thought so? Anyway, we have tournaments where we play other teams from other rec centers and then we go out afterwards and have a soda or something to eat and all of us go, you know, the group. We talk about the game and brag about ourselves and each other. Some of the guys are my friends and lots of the girls are my friends, at least I think so. And some of the guys are kind of cute, but so far I haven't felt as if I needed to "belong" to one of them or go find a secret place in the gym to play "hide-and-go-kiss." And, even weirder—I feel totally and completely there with this group, especially when I'm really playing well. And they compliment me afterwards, you know? Like "Oh, you really kicked 'em, they didn't have a chance" and stuff like like that? I really like it. It really feels good.

What do you think? Do you think that I can be okay without a quote unquote boyfriend—and that other people will like me and want me to be around them because of me? Do you think being part of this group will be enough for now and I can get back to the boyfriend stuff later if someone special enough for me comes along? Oooh, I really like that idea. Special enough for me. Well, gotta go. Time for volleyball practice.

You did say you really definitely see me, didn't you?

Polluters on Parade

A "Talk Show" Short Play

About Polluters on Parade

Here's your chance to satirize, or hold up to public ridicule in a humorous way, two deserving victims—talk shows and polluters.

Your host for this talk show is Sandy Jessica Raphaella. To represent the real-life character on which she is based, give her a blonde wig and a pair of large red glasses. (Of course, she doesn't have to be based on this real-life talk show hostess. Make her a man, give him a silver wig, and call him Phil . . . Donnaho. Or a dark wig and a mustache and call him Geraldo Riviera. This play should be fun to do; it's fine to take liberties with the characters and then adjust the lines accordingly.) Don't forget Sandy Jessica's ivory (plastic) earrings and plastic cleaner bag.

The character Hugh Killem is a poacher and a slayer of animals, so make his costume as exaggerated as you can. Give him jungle fatigues with (toy) knives hanging all over his jacket. Attach pelts of (fake) fur to his clothes—or hang stuffed animals all over him. He is a caricature—that is, a broad character intended to amuse your audience rather than seem terribly realistic. (Certainly many animals really are slaughtered for the purpose of providing accessories for humans every year—that part is unfortunately quite realistic.)

Pat and Rose are two audience members who ask questions of the guests. Do whatever you like with these two. Make them old, young, loud, or timid, whatever seems like fun. Don't be confined to gender, either—Rose would probably be more sympathetic to the mom if she was indeed a woman also, but not necessarily! Just change her name if you decide to make her a male character. No need to worry about that with Pat, however; everyone knows that the name "Pat" can be for man or woman.

Dr. Bruce Wizenheimer should probably be a stereotypical psychiatrist wearing a jacket with elbow patches and perhaps a pipe. Maybe he has a big stack of reference books on the floor next to him. Maybe he takes notes on a pad of paper throughout the scene.

Di Perkins, mother of twins, is another opportunity for some fun and silly costuming. Maybe she has a tube of baby ointment or a diaper sticking out of a pocket. She should probably look pretty harried, as if she didn't really take time to dress up or do her hair before the show. Maybe she has a squeak toy in her pocket that she sits on accidentally at random.

"John" can look any way at all, but do make the square of black construction paper and have him put it over his eyes as if to disguise his identity. Or you could go a different way with this "sight gag" and put some type of Halloween mask on him.

Mr. and Mrs. Paul Luter should look nice in business wear (after all, they're SO important!). They probably need briefcases (maybe matching!) and maybe some of the disposable items they mention—disposable pens, polystyrene cups, etc.

Exercises to Accompany Polluters on Parade

1. Early in this script, the talk show host "cuts" to go to a commercial. As a class, write a humorous advertisement to go in this slot. (Or divide into small groups and have a competition to see which commercial gets to be presented here.) You may wish to choose a local, currently running commercial and do a humorous version of it. This is called "spoofing," or, in easier terms, "making fun of." Be sure to choose a commercial with which everyone is familiar. Or you may wish to "start from scratch" and write an ad for some silly product. (The humor may lie in the product or service being sold—or the person doing the selling. Is there some celebrity who would look very foolish selling a certain item?) Your original commercial needs to be only a minute or two in length.

2. Many of the characters in this short play are "caricatures," or characters whose traits are exaggerated for comic value rather than to seem perfectly realistic. The visual artist does the same thing with charcoal or chalk when he draws a caricature of a subject—that is, he takes certain aspects of the subject's appearance and exaggerates them on paper the way a playwright exaggerates them on stage.

   With that thought in mind, create other caricatures. What about an overprotective parent? How would he or she behave? What about a shy, retiring accountant stereotype or caricature? How would he or she talk? How would he or she dress? Discuss as a class.

3. Think about yourself for a moment. If a person were to draw a caricature of you, what features would be exaggerated? How about if a playwright featured a caricature of you in a play? What would you be like? What traits or habits, physical or vocal, do you have which could be exaggerated for comic effect? Write a brief scene featuring yourself as a caricature.

4. Though this play is broad in its comedy, it still communicates an important message—that we may be ruining the only world we have. Do you think you are more aware of the environment and conservation than you were, say, three years ago? As a class, discuss habits which have already changed. (Do you throw away an aluminum soda can without a thought now, or do you look around for a recycling bin without even thinking about it? Do your newspapers at home go into the trash or somewhere else?) Add to your discussion things that you could do to make an even greater effort. Might your class undertake an environmental project as, for instance, an Earth Day activity? What about a performance of this play, proceeds of which go to Greenpeace or some environmental agency closer to home?

5. A publishing company called Earthworks Press in Berkeley, California, has many publications which can provide more information about recycling and conservation, many of which are written especially for young people. The address is 1400 Shattuck Ave., #25, Berkeley, CA 94709. The phone number is 510.841.5866, fax number 510.841.7121. The publications in the list on the following page can all be ordered from Earthworks.

50 Simple Things You Can Do To Save The Earth. Shows simple things anyone can do to protect Earth.

The Recycler's Handbook. A guide to recycling all materials, including glass, paper, plastics, and more.

Kid Heroes of the Environment: Simple Things Real Kids Are Doing to Save the Earth. Features success stories about real-life kids, ages 7 to 15, who are working to save Earth. Each story contains a biography of the child, a description of the project, and sources for further information. (This might be a good source for an idea for an environmental project for your class.)

The Student Environmental Action Guide. This book was written by the Student Environmental Action Coalition (SEAC), and it is about how to make eco-changes on campus. It's really for high school and college campuses, but surely the changes would work at the middle school level as well.

50 Simple Things Kids Can Do To Save The Earth. This is the students' version of *50 Simple Things* mentioned above. It's filled with fun tips and experiments that show kids how to help save the planet.

Cast

(in order of appearance)

Sandy Jessica Raphaella, a talk show host
Hugh Killem, poacher
Pat, an audience member
Dr. Bruce Wizenheimer, psychiatrist
Di Perkins, mother of twins
Rose, an audience member
"John"
Mr. Paul Luter
Mrs. Luter
Stagehands

Polluters on Parade

A "Talk Show" Short Play for Several Boys and Girls

(The play begins with Sandy center stage. Behind her, the guests are seated in semicircular talk show fashion.)

Sandy: Good evening, unemployed people of America, so glad you have your television sets on this afternoon. I'm Sandy Jessica Raphaella, and welcome to our show. Our topic today—Polluters on Parade. We'll be talking with several enemies of Earth's environment today and giving me, Sandy Jessica Raphaella, an opportunity to nail 'em. I mean, to ask them pertinent questions and gain insight into what makes a polluter . . . pollute! We'll be right back after this message:

(Insert original television commercial spoof here.)

Sandy: We're back. You know, my red glasses have become something of a trademark, but they were not always my spectacles of choice. I used to have a very lovely, very expensive pair of tortoiseshell glasses—but at some point, I stopped buying tortoiseshell. Why did I do this? I'll turn to our first guest for that answer. He's a poacher by trade, and a slayer of innocent animals—please help me welcome Mr. Hugh Killem. Mr. Killem, welcome to the program.

Hugh: Thank you, Sandy. Nice ivory earrings.

Sandy: They're *plastic*, thank you very much.

Hugh: Sorry—I didn't realize you were so cheap.

Sandy: Mr. Killem, you slaughter hundreds of animals every year for the express purpose of selling their pelts and body parts to make expensive items for people to wear! Now, what do you have to say for yourself?

Hugh: Well, you know, a man's gotta make a living.

Sandy: That's all you have to say in your defense? You're not even going to try to cop out with the old "they would've died eventually anyway" excuse?

Hugh: No, but hey, Sandy, that's a good one! They were all gonna die eventually, so I just, you know, moved things up a little bit. Sometimes with traps, sometimes with bullets.

(An audience member shouts and waves his or her hand.)

Sandy: Yes, you have a question for Mr. Killem?

Pat: I think you're terrible, you poacher you! Look at those boots! Are they alligator?

Hugh: Don't insult me! They're the finest eel money can buy.

Pat: Aw, you're the eel, you slimy outfit. Slither back where you came from!

(Sits back down.)

Sandy: Let's see if we can shed some light on why Mr. Killem would do the things he does. Our next guest is a psychiatrist who specializes in destructive behavior. He usually focuses his attention on politics, but he's here with us today to discuss polluters. Please welcome Dr. Bruce Wizenheimer.

Dr. Wizenheimer: Hello, Sandy, nice of you to have me on the show.

Sandy: Thank you for coming, doctor. Now, talk to me about Hugh Killem! Why does he slaughter animals who are clearly in danger of becoming extinct?

Dr. Wizenheimer: Let me see if I can explain this to you in a concise way. When Mr. Killem was a little boy, his parents wouldn't allow him to have a cat or any other kind of pet, is that right Mr. Killem?

Hugh: Not at all. We raised Siamese cats, and I had a special one named Brynner who slept by my bed each night.

Dr. Wizenheimer: I see. Well, when he was walking home from school one day, a stray dog must have jumped out and barked at him ferociously, scaring him half to death.

Hugh: I don't remember such a thing happening. In fact, I lived very close to my elementary school and generally rode my bike to and from school. I don't remember anything scary ever happening.

Dr. Wizenheimer *(pauses, then)*: It must have been a fishing accident then. You were peering over the edge of a boat into the water when a fish flopped up, causing you to become distracted and fall overboard.

Hugh: Never happened.

Dr. Wizenheimer *(pauses again, then)*: It's the money.

Hugh: Why didn't you just ask me?

Sandy: Moving on to our next guest . . . she's a housewife, mother of twins, and the author of the article "Why Is Everything in My House Sticky?" which was recently published in *Crumb Grabber Magazine.* Please give a warm welcome to Di Perkins. Mrs. Perkins, how are you?

Di: I'm fine, and I have no idea why I'm here. I'm a humble little mother who never hurt anyone, especially not an animal.

Sandy: I'm sure you don't realize it, Mrs. Perkins, but let's discuss your children. What is their age?

Di: They're five months old.

Sandy: And they take up a lot of your time, don't they?

Di *(sarcastically)*: Oh, no! I still have time to garden, sculpt, and stencil designs on the furniture!

Sandy: So you like to buy products that help save time for you?

Di: Yes, of course. Say, is this leading somewhere? 'cause, speaking of time, I've got a sitter on the clock . . .

Sandy: So, Mrs. Perkins, you use disposable bottle liners and disposable baby wipes and, the worst offender of all, disposable diapers, am I right?

Di: Hey, wait a minute! I'm a harried, frazzled mother!

Sandy: Are you aware, Mrs. Perkins, that it takes the soil of the earth hundreds of years to decompose the materials that make up disposable diapers? And what about those cute tiny baby food jars, Mrs. Perkins? Do you recycle that glass?

Di: Do I recycle glass? I don't have time to brush my hair, much less run to the recycling center!

(An audience member stands up.)

Sandy: Yes, you have a question?

Rose: I just want to say that I think y'all are being too hard on Mrs. Perkins. I mean, the woman's got twins! I say anything she can do to make her life a little easier, she ought to do!

Di: Thank you for understanding my side.

Rose: However, I do think she could use cloth diapers occasionally. And call your city sanitation department! They may have curbside recycling. Many cities do. And what about a warm cloth for baby cleaning? Even Mother Earth deserves a break today!

Di: Okay, okay, stop nagging! I'll look into some of this stuff.

Sandy: Thank you, Di. And start saving now for college.

Di: Ouch.

Sandy: Now it's time to welcome our next guest—he's asked to be called simply . . . "Mr. Doe."

Mr. Doe *(Mr. Doe has a black strip of paper in front of his eyes)*: Hello, Sandy.

Sandy: Why are you here, Mr. Doe? What's your crime against nature?

Mr. Doe: I . . . I honestly don't know. I recycle, I bundle up my newspapers . . . I remove the slicks . . . which is more than I can say for most of our gasoline companies these days. I have a low-flow showerhead which reduces the amount of water that comes out of my shower, and I have planted so many trees in my front yard I accidentally drive by my house most of the time because I can't see it.

Sandy *(pauses dramatically)*: And in the mornings, Mr. Doe?

Mr. Doe: What?

Sandy: What do you do when you're getting ready for work in the morning?

Mr. Doe: Well, I take a nice, hot shower . . .

Sandy: Ah ha!

Mr. Doe *(putting his hand over his mouth)*: That's it! My long, hot showers in which I sing show tunes at the top of my lungs!

Sandy: That's probably noise pollution in itself.

Mr. Doe: Hey!

Sandy: And what about shampoo and soap? Are they fragrance-free and natural?

Mr. Doe: No. No, I'll confess it. I use *Wow! That's LILAC!* brand shampoo and conditioner and a soap called *Everything's Sudsing up Roses*. They're full of fragrance and I never even thought about it! Thank you, Sandy, for showing me the error of my ways. I'm off to Real Man Hardware to buy a low-flow showerhead to cut my water use in half. And maybe I'll stop singing! Thanks, Sandy! And Happy Earth Day to you!

Sandy: Some days are more rewarding than others.

Mr. Luter: Excuse me, Sandy, could I speak my piece?

Sandy: Of course. We have a married couple here today. Mr. and Mrs. Paul Luter. Welcome to the program, Luters.

Mrs. Luter: Thank you, Sandy. I'm sad to say we've never been able to see your show even once on television.

Mr. Luter: That's right. My wife and I are so busy, so *important,* that we never, ever watch television. We're always on the go, rush rush rush! Isn't that right, darling?

Mrs. Luter: I'm afraid so. But we did take time out from our busy, important schedule today to chat with you for a moment about our lifestyle. We use disposable, convenient things, and we're proud of it.

Mr. Luter: That's right. I shave with a disposable razor and throw it in the trash.

Mrs. Luter: I have a confession to make! Sometimes I shave my legs with your razors!

Mr. Luter: You don't! You vixen!

Mrs. Luter: I'm afraid I do, when I'm taking a really long, luxurious shower with my favorite fragrance of shampoo. Or body wash. Or sometimes even a bubble bath, if I get up really early!

Anyway, smelling all fresh and artificially scented, I head for the kitchen where I prepare coffee using bleached white filters. Then I pour our morning coffee in polystyrene cups that we can take with us in our cars. We're in such a hurry, you see! We're so important!

Mr. Luter: I pop a disposable ballpoint pen in my pocket and head off to work.

Mrs. Luter: I wish we could ride together, but we work in separate parts of town!

Mr. Luter: I would like to tell you that we turn off every light before we leave our home . . .

Mrs. Luter: And that we turn our air conditioner to a warmer temperature when we leave for the day.

Mr. Luter: Or our heater to a cooler temp in the winter.

Mrs. Luter: But I'm afraid that's not true! We go flying out of the house at such a rate of speed, we're doing well if we remember to lock the front door!

Mr. Luter: We're horrible!

Mrs. Luter: Oh, and let me tell you about when I shop for groceries!

Mr. Luter: This is too much!

Mrs. Luter: I actually own some of those dear little cloth bags—but I never remember to take them to the store! They're in my kitchen, hiding from me in a drawer! I just end up loading my trunk with plastic bags full of groceries! I'm terrible!

Mr. Luter: But the worst thing she does—and I'm guilty too!— is buying food that is wrapped in not one, not two, but *several* layers of plastic!

Mrs. Luter: You know, like fish frozen on those little polystyrene trays and then wrapped up so they'll stay fresh?

Mr. Luter: They do stay fresh, but our whole trash is full of polystyrene and plastic wrap!

Mrs. Luter: I can only imagine what our city dump must look like.

Mr. Luter: We're terrible! But it's just that we're so busy, and so very important in our jobs . . .

(Sandy has been growing more and more agitated as she listens to the Luters, and finally she can't bear it any longer. She jumps up, produces a plastic cleaner bag and approaches the Luters menacingly.)

Sandy: I've heard enough! The two of you deserve to be parked on a polystyrene tray and shrinkwrapped!

Dr. Wizenheimer: Sandy, stop! That cleaner bag is not a toy!

Sandy *(coming to her senses)*: You're right—what was I thinking? My career could've become an endangered species. Would somebody get these two polluters off my set before I mount their heads on my wall?

(as stage hands escort them away)

Mrs. Luter: I never!

Mr. Luter: We were just trying to give a conflicting point of view!

Mrs. Luter: We didn't really even have time to be here!

Mr. Luter: We're really busy . . .

Mrs. Luter: And really important!

Sandy: Not as important as the planet, Bozos, and don't you forget it. Well, this has been interesting and informative, everyone, and thanks for tuning in. This is Sandy Jessica Raphaella, saying remember—you bet your boots—you shouldn't pollute.

Hugh: Are we back to my boots again? That eel was sick, I tell you. He had made out his last will and testament . . .

Sandy: Join us tomorrow when our guests will be alien beings who have infiltrated Earth as . . . talk show hosts? What? Who okayed this? Until then, so long, America!

OOOOOOOOOO Cheerleader Tryouts

A Humorous Duet for Two Girls

Cheerleader Tryouts

A Humorous Duet for Two Girls

(The scene begins just after cheerleader tryouts have concluded. Tiffany and Heather run in, out of breath and tired.)

Heather: Oh, Tiffany, I watched you try out! You were GREAT, I'm not kidding.

Tiffany: Oh, Heather, I wasn't, I was HORRIBLE! I'm so embarrassed I could die. I will never be a cheerleader for John Glenn High School, home of the mighty fighting Astronauts!

Heather and Tiffany *(cheering)*: All right!

Tiffany: You were the one who was good! I watched you, too! You were really coordinated and athletic looking!

Heather: What are you talking about? You put everybody else to shame, I mean it.

Tiffany: I didn't put anybody else to shame except myself! I was terrible!

Heather: You were fabulous!

Tiffany: I was awful!

Heather: You were the best by far!

Tiffany: I was . . . *(a pause)* . . . really?

Heather: Yes!

Tiffany: I didn't look spastic and like I was tripping around over my own two feet?

Heather: No!

Tiffany: I didn't look like I forgot the cheer and had no rhythm or school spirit?

Heather: The opposite of that! I swear!

Tiffany: Oh! *(looking a little happy and relieved)*

Heather: I'm telling you right now, nobody noticed that one little tiny mess-up.

Tiffany: What little tiny mess-up?

Heather: The one when you were supposed to turn to the right and face the statue of John Glenn? . . .

Tiffany: The one that's suspended from the ceiling as if he were in space?

Heather: Yes . . . and you turned to the left for just a tiny second . . .

Tiffany: Oh no!

Heather: But no one noticed, I'm sure! It was really quick! And I only noticed because I'm such a good friend of yours and was watching your every move!

Tiffany: No, I'm doomed! If you saw, then the judges did too! I'm ruined.

Heather: I promise you it was not noticeable. Neither was . . . oh, never mind.

Tiffany: Heather, what! What else did I do wrong?

Heather: It was really nothing.

Tiffany: Tell me!

Heather: Well, there was that time you turned a cartwheel and your legs weren't perfectly straight.

Tiffany *(gasps, horrified)*: Bendy legs in a cartwheel?

Heather: They only looked a little bit like frog legs. I'm sure no one noticed.

Tiffany *(even more horrified)*: Frog legs! Oh great. I'm going back in there right now and tell them to take my name out of the running. I'll never make it and I'm humiliated.

Heather: Tiffany, now I feel terrible. I shouldn't have said anything.

Tiffany: Don't be silly, how else will I know if my good friends don't tell me? What would I do without you!

Heather: How sweet of you to say!

Tiffany: Just tell me this. How did my backflip look?

Heather: It looked . . . almost perfect!

Tiffany: Almost? What did I do wrong?

Heather: Almost nothing!

Tiffany: Heather . . . tell me right now. I can take it.

Heather: Well . . . oh, I feel so mean!

Tiffany: Come on. It will only be mean if you keep it from me.

Heather: Well, when your feet touched the ground the last time . . . it was . . .

it was kind of like your neck snapped like a whiplash, you know, like this. *(She does a very uncoordinated and unflattering imitation of Tiffany with her head flying backward).*

Tiffany *(beside herself with horror)*: Oh my heavens!

Heather: Well, I mean, not as bad as that, you know, but sort of.

Tiffany: That's it. I'm going in there and telling them to forget it. I am so humiliated! What was I thinking to even try out? I am uncoordinated and a klutz. Thank you, Heather, for your honesty. Some friends wouldn't have been so frank.

Heather: I feel bad!

Tiffany: No, don't! You saved me a lot of humiliation. I'll see you tomorrow in class! *(She exits.)*

Heather: Bye bye! *(looks after her, smiles)* Well. One good friend down, seven more to go. *(sees someone off stage)* Mitzie! I was watching you try out for cheerleader! You were great! Oh, except for one little thing . . .

WE TWO KINGS

A Historical Duet about Coretta Scott King and Martin Luther King

About WE TWO KINGS

One of the greatest, most influential, and peace-loving men of all times was the Reverend Dr. Martin Luther King. His death in 1968 shocked the nation and left a void that would never be filled.

We Two Kings is a duet acting scene between Dr. King and his wife, Coretta Scott King. As in our other historical dramatizations, artistic liberties have been taken with their words—we certainly don't know how the Kings spoke together, or whether they teased each other. But there was most assuredly a loyalty and a closeness there, as is evidenced by the way each regarded the other throughout their time together and by the way Mrs. King continued Dr. King's work after his death.

As with the short play *What, Watergate?* you may wish to turn this from a duet into a short play by including other actors acting out the events that the Kings describe. Why not create a chorus of singers to provide background music? Certainly the church played a large role in Dr. King's life. The music of the church must have underscored much that he did and accomplished.

This would be a wonderful class project—maybe for the third Monday in January?

Exercises to Accompany WE TWO KINGS

1. Be sure you know the meaning of the following words before starting to work on this duet acting scene:

   implore
   industrious
   activist
   boycott

2. When Coretta asks her audience to "carry our torch," Martin makes a joke about not realizing that she was an Olympic runner. What did Coretta really mean? What was Martin's joke?

3. What were the "Jim Crow" laws? See if you can find out at your local library or from your history teacher whether they were official, legal, voted-upon laws, or just a common understanding between groups of people. F.Y.I.—as late as the early 1960s in Dallas, Texas, one could enter a public laundromat and see a sign that read "Whites Only." Did that refer to the clothing that could be washed there? Or the people who could wash their clothes there?

4. Have you ever had an experience in which you were forbidden to associate with someone because of something over which you had no control, such as your race, religion, the part of town in which you live, etc? How did this make you feel? Write a brief paper describing your feelings or discuss the experience with the class.

5. The very courageous Rosa Parks is mentioned in this scene. How courageous must she have been to do what she did aboard that bus! Write a brief scene in which you portray the role of Rosa Parks. Be "inside her head" as she becomes more and more frustrated as blacks move to the back of the bus and begin giving up even those seats. What thoughts must she have had right before she said "no" to the driver? What images might have flickered through her mind that changed her mind—and history—forever? We have no way to know these answers—just use your imagination and fill in the historical blanks as you think it might have been.

WE TWO KINGS

A Historical Duet about Coretta Scott King and Martin Luther King

Martin: Hello everyone. My name is Martin Luther King, Jr. And this is my beautiful wife, Coretta Scott King.

Coretta: So lovely to see all of you today.

Martin: Coretta and I are here through the magic of theatre and imagination to visit with you today and tell you how we feel and have always felt—that men and women of all colors and backgrounds should be able to move about freely and equally and enjoy this wonderful land in which we live.

Coretta: Martin and I dedicated our lives to this idea and want to implore you to continue this attitude. To carry our torch, so to speak.

Martin: Why, Coretta, I knew you were a great singer, but I didn't know you were an Olympic runner!

Coretta: Hush, you silly man.

Martin: Let's tell our story, shall we?

Coretta: Martin was born in Atlanta, Georgia, on January 15, 1929.

Martin: It was a time when there were good things in the country . . . and there were bad things. Like the Jim Crow laws.

Coretta: These laws separated white people from black people, especially in places like restaurants and hotels. There were certain public places which black people couldn't even enter!

Martin: There were drinking fountains with signs that said "Whites Only."

Coretta: I remember going into a drugstore and asking for an ice cream cone. I had to enter through the side door, not the front door . . .

Martin: And they made her take the flavor that they had too much of!

Coretta: So this was the way of things when Martin Luther King, Jr. was born, the son of a minister at the Ebenezer Baptist Church in Atlanta, Georgia.

Martin: I remember playing baseball with two neighbor boys who happened to be white. One day they weren't outside when I showed up with my bat and ball. I went to their house, and their mother told me that we could never play together again because they were white. Because we were different colors! I went home and cried.

Coretta: But Martin's mother was a good woman, and wise! She explained to Martin about slavery and about how some people continued to hold onto ideas about black people that weren't right. She taught Martin to read.

Martin: And read I did! I believed—and I still do—that education and knowledge are tremendous tools that can be used against hatred and ignorance. I decided to be twice as smart and twice as good a person as anyone else.

Coretta: While Martin was busy learning and making his plans, I was growing up in Perry County, Alabama. The first nine years of my life were spent in a two-room home with bare floors and peeling paper on the walls. There were three of us children, and it was fairly crowded!

Martin: They had no running water—they carried it in from the well in the backyard.

Coretta: I guess you could say it was "running" water—some days we surely must've run in with it!

Martin: Now who's being silly?

Coretta: My father worked very hard at several jobs, and we finally had enough money to move to a six-room house. My sister and I each had our own bedroom, there was a living room—we thought it was a mansion!

Martin: But there was soon trouble.

Coretta: Yes. My father was the only black man in Perry County who owned a truck. He was stopped often as he drove to and from work—one of his jobs was to haul lumber for a mill operator. He was told to stop working in the area. When he refused, somebody burned down our fine new home. I think it was that day that I decided to see if I couldn't make a difference in the way people thought of black people and the way in which they were treated.

Martin: Education continued to be very important to both Coretta and me. When Coretta was little, there was only one schoolhouse for black children, three miles from their home. They walked there and back every day. No buses were provided for the black children.

Coretta: And the only high school for blacks was twenty miles away. But my father converted a truck into a bus and drove all the children from the area to and from school. So I got to graduate from high school.

Martin: And I entered Morehouse College at the age of fifteen.

Coretta: You smart fella!

Martin: I had thought that I would be a doctor, then a lawyer. But finally I decided that continuing my father's work as a minister was my true calling. I preached my first sermon at the Ebenezer Baptist Church at age seventeen.

Coretta: My industrious husband worked the whole time he was at school, in different jobs.

Martin: I worked in the stockroom of a mattress factory. I worked at a shipping company loading and unloading trains and trucks and at a post office sorting mail. In the fall of 1951, I entered Boston University to study for my doctorate—and met someone who would change my life forever.

Coretta: Your history teacher?

Martin: Nope.

Coretta: The quarterback of the BU football team?

Martin: Nope.

Coretta: Your humble but beautiful wife-to-be?

Martin: The very woman. Coretta was studying music at the New England Conservatory of Music. She had the voice of an angel.

Coretta: I think you're prejudiced in my favor, Dr. King! But I did love to sing, and had been very lucky to win a scholarship to Antioch College where I wanted to become certified to be a teacher. But guess what? The school board refused to accept me as a practice teacher. I appealed to the president of the college and was told that I would have to teach in a private school. Again my race kept me from doing what I wanted to do!

Martin: But you didn't give in, did you, Coretta?

Coretta: I was tempted to. But I thought to myself, "Now, I'm going to be black the rest of my life, and I have to face these problems. I'm not going to let this one get me down." That's when I joined several committees and student groups concerned with equal rights for black people. I was determined to make a difference.

Martin: After Antioch College, you went to the New England Conservatory of Music in Boston . . .

Coretta: Where I was poor as a churchmouse! I ate peanut butter, graham crackers, and fruit, and that was about it!

Martin: But then you met a man who would change your life forever . . .

Coretta: The man who gave me a job at a mail-order house?

Martin: Nope.

Coretta: The guy across the hall who practiced his trombone until all hours and kept me awake?

Martin: Nope.

Coretta: Oh, that Martin Luther King, Jr., guy they told me about? The one who was studying to be a minister!

Martin: That's the guy!

Coretta: I didn't want to meet you at first! I thought if you were studying to be a minister you'd be all stuck-up and, you know, a "goody two shoes."

Martin: You never told me that!

Coretta: It's true! But then I talked to you on the phone, and then we had a date, and, you know . . .

Martin: No, tell us!

Coretta: I . . . kinda liked you.

Martin: I wanted to marry you right away and you kept stalling!

Coretta: That's true. I wanted to be a concert singer, not the wife of a preacher. But the more we talked, the more I realized that many of our goals were the same. And I thought we could do more good together than we could apart. Besides, I kinda liked you.

Martin: We were married in June of 1953 on the front lawn of your parents' home in Alabama.

Coretta: And then it was time for Martin to get to work as a minister. He decided to work "down south" as the pastor of the Dexter Avenue Baptist Church in Montgomery, Alabama. This was an area that really needed some eye-opening about equality!

Martin: I'll say. In December of 1955, something happened on a bus that would change the world forever.

Coretta: You're thinking of Rosa Parks.

Martin: I am.

Coretta: See, in those days, those Jim Crow law days, blacks had to rely on public transportation—you know, buses—to get to their jobs. Many did not have cars. Blacks had to ride at the back of the bus always, and if the bus got crowded, a black had to give up whatever seat he might have if a white person didn't have one.

Martin: But this one day, there was a woman named Rosa Parks. She got on a bus in Montgomery, Alabama, where I was working as a minister. She took a seat in the middle of the bus, just behind the "whites only" section. At every stop, more and more people got on . . .

Coretta: Until finally every seat was taken. The driver told Rosa and three other black riders to get up. The others did. Rosa refused.

Martin: The driver pulled over and left the bus. He came back with a policeman.

Coretta: Rosa Parks was arrested.

Martin: The next morning, I got a call from a civil rights activist named Mr. E. D. Nixon who asked me to help organize a one-day boycott of all the buses in Montgomery.

Coretta: You know what a boycott is, right? Where a whole group refuses to do something. To make a point.

Martin: We decided to join in and set the date for December 5.

Coretta: What a time! I had just had my first child, Yolanda, and I was trying to take care of her, yet the phone kept ringing! At six o'clock the next morning, Martin and I looked out the window. A bus was going by—and it was completely empty! The boycott had actually happened!

Martin: It took almost a year from the time Rosa Parks refused to give up her seat, but finally the U.S. Supreme Court ruled that Jim Crow laws were against United States law, and ordered them repealed.

Coretta: At six o'clock on the morning of December 21, 1956, Martin got on a Montgomery bus. The white bus driver smiled and said, "We are glad to have you this morning."

Martin: We had made a difference.

Coretta: But what a hard year! Our home was bombed one night.

Martin: Imagine how I felt! I rushed into my home to make sure my wife and baby were safe, which they were.

Coretta: And he stood out on the lawn and told the crowd that had gathered, "If you have weapons, take them home. We must meet violence with nonviolence. We must love our white brothers. We must meet hate with love."

Martin: There was still much to be done. I wrote a book called *Stride Toward Freedom,* and one day when I was in a department store in New York City, autographing copies of it, a woman came up to me.

Coretta: She asked him if he was Dr. King.

Martin: When I answered yes, she took out a letter opener from her purse and stabbed me.

Coretta: We didn't know it right then, but the letter opener was right next to his heart. If he had sneezed . . .

Martin: Luckily, I wasn't allergic . . .

Coretta: Or even panicked and moved suddenly it would've pierced his heart.

Martin: The doctors patched me up that time, though.

Coretta: But Martin didn't stop or even slow down. He and several other black leaders formed the Southern Christian Leadership Conference, called the SCLC. They traveled throughout the country, speaking and trying to make changes.

Martin: People all over the country were trying to make changes, not just me. For instance, there were still lunch counters in the South at which black people were not allowed to sit. In February, 1960, a few black students sat at one and asked to be served. When they were refused, they wouldn't leave. Other students joined them. These came to be called "sit-ins," and I took part in a few myself.

Coretta: And you were arrested a few times, I might add.

Martin: I spent more than one night in jail, it's true. The worst one was when you were pregnant with our third child and had two small children at home.

Coretta: But I received a call from someone who helped us very much. I think his name was "John F." somebody . . .

Martin: Kennedy, I'm thinking.

Coretta: That's the one. He asked after the health of the family and told me that he would do anything he could to help me. The next day, you were released from jail.

Martin: We not only "sat in," we also marched. The biggest and most successful of these was on August 28, 1963, when two hundred thousand people, black and white alike, joined together to march to Washington. I gave a speech to them from the steps of the Lincoln Memorial. It started, "I have a dream."

Coretta: Martin was chosen Man Of The Year by Time magazine in 1963. And in 1964, he won the Nobel Peace Prize, a great honor. He was the youngest man ever to win that prize.

Martin: Of course, the end came for me on April 4, 1968, when James Earl Ray fired a shotgun at me from the window of a house in Memphis, Tennessee. That was the end for me, but not for Coretta, who kept the dream alive.

Coretta: I can't tell you how hard it was, but I kept going. I sang at fund-raising events. I launched the Poor People's Campaign from Memphis, something Martin had started but now would not be able to finish. I spoke at many, many gatherings. I oversaw the opening of the Martin Luther King, Jr. Center for Social Change in Atlanta, where it all began for Martin.

Martin: Remember us, not just on Martin Luther King Day, but all days. Remember that, if you have a dream, don't let it die. Dream it—and do it. I had a dream . . . and it went like this. "I have a dream that one day on the red hills of Georgia the sons of former slaves and the sons of former slave owners will be able to sit down together at the table of brotherhood."

Coretta: "I have a dream that my four children will one day live in a nation where they will not be judged by the color of their skin but by the content of their character."

Martin and Coretta: We have a dream today. Keep it alive, won't you?

The Dan and John Duet

A Humorous Duet for Two Boys

About The Dan and John Duet

The Dan and John Duet is a scene for two boys who are of different ethnic backgrounds and become good friends. You decide which character is which ethnicity. It's really up to you, and will be dictated, obviously, by the actors available to play the parts.

There are several places in the scene where you can "personalize" the dialogue to make it more fun for you and your audience. These include the local "public broadcast" station and the name of your rival school and its team name. The sport doesn't have to be basketball. Change it to football, if you like, and make the big play an interception at the twenty-yard line.

There are also some places to make the dialogue more representative of the ethnic origin of the characters. It's very important to keep the use of ethnic-specific foods, etc., in a fun and nonderogatory context. The whole point of the scene is that no matter what our background, there is a common area on which we can meet (sometimes the school cafeteria!) and become friends working toward a common goal. So, when they start talking about the fact that they are "different," John says, "His idea of a big meal is ________." If he's a Caucasian boy, it might be a Big Mac. (Or perhaps Dan is a Caucasian boy from the state of Texas, in which case he might enjoy a big, juicy steak.) And so on.

You can also change these names, if you like! John may become Juan if that character is Hispanic. Or leave it John—many boys of many backgrounds are named John. Following the "politically correct" line about Christmas, you could add a line that mentions Hanukkah for the other boy to say.

This scene lends itself to some good work in timing and on-stage chemistry and rapport. One boy needs to begin speaking almost before the other boy has finished his line to tighten up the pacing of the scene. It is very important that we see the fondness and respect between the two boys. Even when they are teasing each other, there is affection there which must be evident.

The Dan and John Duet

A Humorous Duet for Two Boys

Dan: Hi, my name is Dan and I'm here today to tell you an amazing story.

John: Not amazing as in "America's Most Amazing New Inventions" amazing . . . .

Dan: But almost. Only you don't have to turn on Channel _____ *(Insert local Public Broadcast Station or cable station such as "The Discovery Channel.")* to see it, you just have to sit right where you are.

John: It's about me. John.

Dan: Yeah, it's about this guy John here. And me. And how I changed my mind about something.

John: Emotional violin music please!

Dan: Don't get your hankies out yet, let me just tell you. See, I play basketball for my school. And I'm really, really good.

John: I think probably one "really" will do the trick there, Dan.

Dan: Yeah, yeah . . . anyway, the problem is, I'm not really, really good—or even really good . . . in math.

John: He's pathetic!

Dan: I'm pathetic.

John: I, however, am really, really good in math because I work in my parents' store. I've always had to make change for customers, figure out how much stuff should cost after we mark it up, figure tax percentages, etc., etc. I'm a math whiz. I'm amazing. I'm . . .

Dan: Okay, okay . . . he can add one and one. Now, go back in time with us. It was the first six weeks after the winter holidays.

John: I'm so impressed that you were politically correct, Dan, and didn't say "Christmas!"

Dan: Thank you, thank you. *(He bows.)* The big game was coming up between __________ *(Insert your school name here.)* and our most bitter enemies, the __________ *(Insert rival team name here.)* of __________. *(Insert rival school name here.)*

John: Wait, Dan, I'm confused. Do you mean they are actually bitter? Like they're really mean and mad at the world? Or do you mean that they have a bitter taste? Like when you're a little kid . . .

Dan: Pay no attention to the boy behind the calculator. May I continue?

John: Please.

Dan: So the game was coming up, a math test was coming up, and my grades were not coming up. In fact, they were plummeting.

John: Great word!

Dan: Thank you.

John: Plummeting. "The elevator was plummeting when its cable snapped. Shoppers were screaming . . ."

Dan: John.

John: Sorry. Please go on.

Dan: So I'm at lunch one day, trying to eat something that the lunchroom tried to pass off as a cheeseburger while I looked over some sample problems in my math book.

John: He was dripping all over the pages of his book. No wonder he's failing. He can't read the problems! He can't see the problems for the cheese, sort of.

Dan: Oooh, that was bad. Anyway, John comes and sits down next to me and just stares at me.

John: We didn't know each other.

Dan: No. Now don't misunderstand this, or start looking up how to spell "racist" or anything, but as you can see, John and I are . . .

John: Different colors.

Dan: Yeah.

John: We come from different ethnic backgrounds.

Dan: Yeah.

John: His idea of a big meal is __________. *(Insert a meal which Dan would probably enjoy.)*

Dan: Whereas John would rather dine on __________. *(Insert a food John would enjoy.)*

John: But neither one of us would consider cafeteria food any treat.

Dan: You got that right. Anyway, he sits down and starts staring at me and I finally notice him and, like, bark at him.

John: Something like, "What are you looking at?"

Dan: I was kinda mean. But I was nervous and scared about the test . . .

John: And about the cheeseburger plummeting into your digestive system.

Dan: Yeah, that too. At first I tried to get rid of him.

John: But I wouldn't go away.

Dan: Why was that, by the way?

John: I'm not sure, really. I thought you needed help.

Dan: I sure did.

John: And then there was that little basketball team detail . . .

Dan: I knew it!

John: So, get on with the story! Tell them how we got to be friends and how I came over to your house every day . . .

Dan: Wait, wait, they'll be confused. Let me tell this in order. I tried very hard to get rid of this guy, and for no good reason. I didn't know any bad stuff about him. He didn't have bad breath. He didn't try to borrow lunch money from me.

John: As if you could've counted it out to me.

Dan: The only reason I tried to ditch him was because . . . well, you know, what I already said. He's a different color.

John: If you went to the paint store and got color chips, we'd be at different ends of the color wheel.

Dan: You even lost me on that one.

John: Sorry.

Dan: Nothing else was wrong with him . . . he was different-looking so I didn't trust him. But he just didn't go away.

John: When he couldn't resist whining about his problem a minute more, he unloaded the whole sad story on me. Big math test—big basketball star—big problem.

Dan: And then out came this "I'm so good at math because I work at my parents store" song and dance. And, believe this or not, he said he'd come over to my house after school and help me!

John: I wasn't due at the store until after dinner . . .

Dan: I usually had basketball practice, but under the circumstances, Coach said I could take a couple of days . . .

John: And so, I charmed his mother into some after-school milk and cookies . . .

Dan: We turned off the TV and locked my little sisters out of my room, and we worked problems and we worked problems . . .

John: And he was so pitiful! He kept trying to find excuses to quit! "Aw, come on, John, old buddy that I just met . . . let's go throw the ball around!"

Dan: I did not. I was dedicated.

John: Hmm. I didn't realize that "dedicated" meant "trying desperately to be excused from."

Dan: So, can you guess how this story turns out? My math test was on Friday of that week, and . . .

John: And he failed it!

Dan: Yeah, I still failed it.

John: But he failed it by much less than he would have!

Dan: I was only five points shy of a passing grade.

John: And when he told his teacher that he had been working really hard with a tutor (that's me), she was impressed. She let him come back after school and take the test again. And this time . . .

Dan: I passed!

John: He passed!

Dan: I got to play that weekend!

John: And we won!

Dan: And I hit the winning shot. It was a three-pointer from the top of the key! Nothin' but net! *(He pantomimes the shot.)*

John: And I was sitting on the first row of the bleachers, cheering on my new friend and student to victory.

Dan: You were not, you were under the bleachers trying to make time with Elizabeth who lives on your street.

John: Oops, I didn't think you'd find that out.

Dan: He still helps me now and then.

John: But only when I'm hungry. His mother makes the most wonderful chocolate chip cookies. Could it be that they aren't sliced from the end of a log of dough?

Dan: They're from scratch.

John: We're friends for life!

Dan: So the moral of this story is . . .

John: "Basketball players are really dumb."

Dan: No, that's not it.

John: "Homemade cookies bring up math grades."

Dan: Maybe. But I think it's more like "Don't judge a book by its cover."

John: Now that's catchy! Did you think that up all by yourself?

Dan: Well . . .

John: Didn't you mean "Don't judge a friend by his color?" That would've been really tender and meaningful and would've taught us all a lesson.

(They start to exit as they continue talking.)

Dan: You know what?

John: No.

Dan *(joking)*: I think our friendship is ending.

John: You know what I think?

Dan: No.

John: It's plummeting.

Dan: Oh man . . .

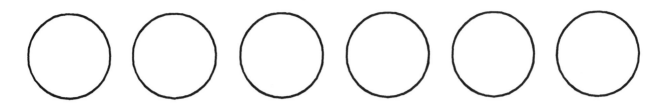

A Mall and the Night Visitors

A Humorous Monologue for a Girl

A Mall and the Night Visitors

A Humorous Monologue for a Girl

(Lou is a soldier. Wear fatigues, if you care to costume, and make a bullet strap out of masking tape and chalk or white crayons. Give her some boots, maybe a toy rifle. And make her real tough. She means business.)

Lou: Hello, privates. Sergeant Lou Tenant here, ready to teach you everything you need to know about one of the most perilous battles you'll ever have to fight. Do I mean the Middle East? Do I mean the streets of downtrodden countries? No sirree Bob, I mean a trip to the local shopping mall at "back to school" time. Believe me, it's not pretty.

Let's start with the parking lot. Now unfortunately, a lot of you new recruits will not have access to your own transportation and will have to rely on enlisted personnel such as the lady who calls herself "your mother"—or even worse, "your big brother or sister." You may have to practice some brainwashing techniques on these individuals to make them see things your way. They may have some idea that this is to be a pleasurable outing, something that will cause the pair of you to bond or share some meaningful experience. Hogwash! You're ready to advance upon the mall, get your back-to-school clothes and perhaps some supplies, and get out without injury or an accidental trip to the video arcade. Discipline is the key.

Now, back to the parking lot. Convince the driver of your transport vehicle that the two of you will never get into the mall unless you find a place to park your American-made automobile. Refuse to be intimidated! Find someone who is lollygagging out to her car like a slow-moving pack mule. Then hover right on her behind until she feels uncomfortable. And if she takes too long loading that stroller into her mini-van, reach over the driver of your vehicle and honk the horn yourself. Your victim will look back at you. Don't be intimidated. Make this face at her *(makes scary, tough-looking face).* That will surely scare her if your honking horn didn't.

Once inside, here are a few land mines of which to be wary. First and foremost, don't you pay a quarter for a paper shopping bag worth one millionth of a cent! The mall pays .09 of a cent for those bags and then they charge 25 or even 30 cents for them! Save that money to put toward a sandwich at the _________ *(Insert humorous mall food shop here.)* if rations run low. Sneak in with a surprise attack, privates: Get a breath mint, a lint-covered sour ball, or a button, and cram it down in that little slot where they want a quarter to go!

Always carry large wads of cotton in your backpack. Stuff this into your ears and you will be spared the brain-numbing effect of repeated torturous exposure to recorded mall music. It is not yet officially documented by the United States Government, but there is reason to believe that listening to instrumental versions of too many show tunes can lead to fatigue and blurring of vision. Be prepared.

Under no circumstances should you allow yourself to be subdued by army personnel taking surveys. If one approaches you, try to escape by using phrases such as "in a hurry" and "not today" or "this is not my native language." If you are forced against your will to stop and answer questions, provide nothing more than name, rank, and serial number. Fairly soon you will be released.

Occasionally you will be called upon to infiltrate the dressing room and actually try on some items of clothing. Move fast—don't look right or left—and never look in the three-way mirror. And above all, wedge your firearm or other rigid object in the handle of the door so that no enemy saleswoman is able to fling it open, exposing you to an entire enemy platoon, shouting her war cry of "How're we doing?"

Now, privates, if I've learned anything in my years of service, it is the following fact: The escalator that you will want (that is, up or down) is never the one next to you in the department store. And you will find that, nine times out of ten, to get over to the one you desire, you have to drop on your belly and dodge sniper fire while sliding your way through china or crystal or other perilous, breakable merchandise. Don't do it! If that escalator is coming down and you want to go up it, just give it one of those little football jogs *(demonstrate)* and run your happy self up the down staircase, growling and making menacing fighting noises like a one-woman swat team. I guarantee you, other soldiers will get out of your way.

That's about all I have to say, except for this important piece of advice passed on to us by other brave officers before me, such as General Patton, General Electric, and General Mills. As often as possible, try to avoid paying cash. Forge ahead bravely and . . . CHARGE!

What? Watergate?

A Historical Monologue (or Short Play) for a Boy

About *What? Watergate?*

The Watergate break-in in the early '70s was an event that changed history forever. Perhaps it's something about which you have heard—but never really understood. This short play will make it a bit more clear.

Though short for a play, it's a little longer than most one-person plays. You may want to experiment with a couple of different production ideas. First, it would be perfectly fine to have the character playing Frank read his script as if from a notebook. Maybe he's been asked to make a speech to the local chapter of . . . the Boy Scouts. Or your history class. Maybe he gets to stand behind a podium and read. If this is to be an acting exercise, however, and not just a speech, he must still adopt a specific character with a specific speech pattern and accent and keep it throughout the play. And he must convince his audience that these are his words and his way of describing the events as he witnessed them.

You might wish to include some other students. As Frank describes certain scenes—the burglars crouched behind the cubicle, the burglars being hauled off to jail, Kent State students protesting—you might have additional actors reenact those scenes in another part of your acting area. Maybe they come onstage and "freeze," creating a tableau effect. Or maybe somebody shoots slides of students acting out these scenes and shows them in class during the presentation.

Be creative and experiment!

Exercises to Accompany *What? Watergate?*

1. At one point in the play, Frank Wills asks his audience to imagine the current president making the statement "I am not a crook." But what if he (or she!) did make that statement? Be a television news reporter, and write a story in which today's president makes the statement that he is not a crook. Create the circumstances in which the statement is made and describe the reaction of the American people.

2. Frank Wills is a real person, actually the night watchman at the Watergate Hotel. In this play, his speech patterns and details of his involvement that night are, however, fiction. In the same spirit, choose an event in history about which you are interested, and create a character who might have been involved. Who was in the room when Martin Luther King decided to say "I have a dream!" Was there an assistant? Or someone even farther removed, like a waiter delivering room service? Whose job was it to gather ink and pens for the signing of the Declaration of Independence? Who put horseshoes on Paul Revere's horse the night he made his famous ride? Write a short monologue telling about a historical event—from someone else's point of view. (Walt Disney's folks do this all the time . . . ever see *Ben and Me* about Benjamin Franklin?)

3. If the Watergate scandal is of interest to you, you might rent a film called *All the President's Men,* starring Dustin Hoffman and Robert Redford. It's based on a book by the same title written by Bob Woodward and Carl Bernstein, the two reporters for the Washington Post who were instrumental in exposing the crimes. Several of the president's aides who were involved have written books of their own. It might be interesting to read one or more of these and get the point of view of those involved on the criminal side. Here's a list of related readings:

Books by Watergate Figures

Blind Ambition by John Dean. New York: Simon and Schuster, 1976.

A Piece of Tape, The Watergate Story: Fact and Fiction by James W. McCord, Jr. Washington, D.C.: Washington Media Services, 1974.

Will: The Autobiography of G. Gordon Liddy by G. Gordon Liddy. New York: St. Martin's Press, 1980.

Witness to Power by John Ehrlichman. New York: Simon and Schuster, 1982.

Books by Reporters

All the President's Men by Carl Bernstein and Bob Woodward. New York: Simon and Schuster, 1974.

The Final Days by Carl Bernstein and Bob Woodward. New York: Simon and Schuster, 1976.

Nightmare: The Underside of the Nixon Years by Anthony Lucas. New York: Viking, 1976.

Reference Books

The End of a Presidency (ed., *The New York Times*). New York: Bantam Books, 1974.

The Presidential Transcripts (ed., *The Washington Post*). New York: Dell, 1974.

The Watergate Hearings: Break-in and Cover-up (ed., *The New York Times*). New York: Viking Press, 1973.

What? Watergate?

A Historical Monologue (or Short Play) for a Boy

(Enter Frank Wills. He is a night watchman, so he may be outfitted with a flashlight on his belt, a notepad and pen, maybe some prop weaponry. He enters, notices an audience, and stops to visit.)

Frank: Well, hello, young people! Frank Wills here. *(He pauses, as though waiting for a response.)* Aw, rats and mice. I keep thinking that one of these times, some audience SOMEWHERE is going to recognize the name and say, "Mr. Wills! Aren't you the one who . . . " But so far, that hasn't happened, and I guess it's gonna be less and less likely as time goes on. I guess I'd better hang onto my American Express card, huh? I "won't leave home without it!"

No, you probably don't know me, but believe it or not, I did change history. Forever. Set in motion a series of events that changed the United States and the way we look at our government and even our president . . . curious now?

Does the name "Watergate" ring a bell for you?

Thought maybe it might. See, I used to work as the night watchman at the Watergate Hotel in Washington, D.C. It was a weird building, because it wasn't just a hotel—it also had offices and apartments in it. Anyhow, one night in June *(he produces a notepad and pen and checks it),* June 17, 1972, to be exact—I have it written down—I was working the night shift, came to work at midnight. Well, as I was making my rounds, I noticed something odd about the lock on the basement door. It was taped over! My first thought was that the building engineer had taped the door open while he was working there so he could get back in without a key if he had to, you know, run to the bathroom or what-not. But in any case, it didn't need to still be taped over at midnight—someone could just come in! So I took the tape off, and I went about my business. So now, at *(consults notebook)* 2:00 a.m., I found myself back in the basement, and guess what? The lock is taped again. Now, Mama Wills didn't raise no fool, boys and girls, and I put two and two together right quick. Somebody had something dishonest in mind—they were taping the lock so that someone could illegally enter that building! I took no chances this time; I called the police.

Three officers of the law arrived at the Watergate right away and started searching the building floor to floor. I went with them to help them out—they appreciated my guidance, I know, even though they kept "shushing" me as I tried to tell them about my experience with the tape. They were dressed in plainclothes, not uniforms. Which is important later on—but let me tell this in order. Anyway, they got to the *(consults notebook)* sixth floor—I have it written down—and found no less than FIVE MEN trying to break into some offices! And they had been trying for thirty minutes! They had apparently not been to Burglary University and taken any courses. In fact, when they had not been able to break the lock on one office, they had taken the door off its hinges! As if that might not have made some folks notice something odd going on!

Anyway, these burglars had a lookout posted with binoculars at the Howard Johnson across the street, but when he saw those long-haired policemen dressed in regular clothes, he thought they were some more bad guys, and didn't warn the burglars that they were coming! So here come the police a-stompin' in. The burglars heard them coming, and so they ducked and hid behind a wooden screen in a cubicle. I followed the cops in and I'll never forget how blamed stupid those burglars looked crouched down there, hoping that we were an all-blind squad of law enforcement officials, I guess, and wouldn't see them hunkered down there. And, let me tell you, they looked nothing like regular burglars—they were in their forties and fifties, wearing business suits and thin rubber gloves, you know like doctors wear? They carried all kinds of equipment too, like walkie-talkies, fancy cameras and film, and bugging equipment. In fact, that was what they were trying to do—put "bugs" in this particular office. You know what "bugs" are, detective fans? Listening devices. Because this particular office belonged to Larry O'Brien, who I'm sure you never heard of either. Mr. O'Brien was the chairman of the Democratic National Committee; that is, the folks who wanted to elect a democrat to the office of president of the United States in 1972. In particular Senator George McGovern, but that's not too important now. The important thing was that these burglars—silly looking though they were with their suits and ties and fancy equipment—were working for some folks . . . who worked for some folks . . . who worked for the guy who was the president of the United States, Richard Milhous Nixon.

Not a good deal.

We didn't know that the president had anything to do with the break-in at the time, though. We just knew that the criminals got hauled off to jail and I didn't get to go along because I had to finish out my shift, but I started to keep my ear to the railroad track about the whole business. I guess I was interested mainly because it had happened in MY HOTEL where I worked, but also just because it didn't look normal. Something seemed off center.

Well, it got pretty weird pretty fast. For instance, one of the burglars was a fella name of James McCord. And he used to work for the CIA—you know, the

Central Intelligence Agency of the U.S. Government. And some people—including this reporter named Woodward who worked for The Washington Post—thought it was really odd that a guy who used to work for the CIA is now breaking and entering the Democrats' office! So Woodward started nosing around—you know how reporters do—and found out that McCord also now worked for a committee that was trying to get President Nixon reelected for a second term! Now this is really not good. What it looked like was that President Nixon's people were bugging the office of the . . . well, the other team. Which was pretty close to right.

How can I explain to you about President Nixon, I wonder? I mean, not that I knew him personally, but as I said, I took careful notice of the whole Watergate business because, really and truly, I started it.

Nixon was a man who worried a lot. He worried that people were trying to "get him." He worried that the Democrats were going to beat him out of the presidency. He worried that the young people of the country felt that he should get America out of that horrible war in Vietnam, which you've probably heard of. And he was absolutely right about that! The young people back then, why they liked to stand up and be counted! So, for instance, in . . . let's see, I think I have it written down . . . 1970 when Nixon decided that the U.S. needed to invade Cambodia, a country right next to Vietnam, to keep the bad guy Vietnamese from getting supplies, he announced this to the country, thinking we'd all say, "Hurray! Bomb some more folks, Tricky Dicky!" But we didn't. Especially the young people. On *(consulting notebook)* May 4, 1970—I have it written down—some kids were protesting—you know, marching around and holding up signs that said things like "Stop the War Now." These particular kids at Kent State University in Ohio got a little bit rowdy, I guess you'd say. Anyhow, some of the Ohio National Guard shot right into that crowd of college kids and killed four of them. Right here in America. Somebody's sons and daughters who hadn't passed their final exams yet, shot dead. So now Nixon was really not popular—not that he pulled those triggers, but he was keeping us involved in this war that nobody wanted to be in.

Like I said, he worried. He worried about the protesters. He worried about whether he would be remembered as a great president who made historical decisions. So he did a lot of things that other presidents hadn't done before him. Like bugging the offices of people he thought were his enemies. And tape recording all the conversations in his own office without telling folks he was taping them.

Not a good deal.

But back to those burglars, locked up in jail. Oh, by the way. One of them had a note in his pocket with the name of Howard Hunt on it. And Mr. Hunt was one of Nixon's right-hand men.

Not a good deal.

Now here's what I think. When folks started to get the idea that the White House had something to do with the whole affair, Nixon shoulda come clean and apologized and gotten on with things. It would've been rough on him, but not as rough as it did turn out. But he didn't do that. He okayed "hush money" to be paid to the burglars—that is, they were paid to keep quiet about the fact that they were working for Nixon's boys—and instructed his right-hand men in how to keep him out of it. AND HE DID THIS WHILE THE TAPES WERE ROLLING IN HIS OWN OFFICE.

Well, I don't have the time or the energy to go through the whole thing and how it all fell apart. But those Washington Post reporters kept investigating away at things and pretty soon it was obvious to the American people that their president had been involved in some illegal dealings. At one point, President Nixon got in trouble about some income taxes that he owed. This didn't have anything to do with Watergate, it was just a bad coincidence. Anyhow, he says right out: "People have got to know whether or not their president is a crook. Well, I'm not a crook." Now what kind of thing is that to be hearing from the president of the United States? What if the president right now was to go on TV and say such a thing? What would you think?

So we watched and we waited and there was a big trial about the whole Watergate business. The president was asked to turn over all the tapes that were recorded in his office that might shed some light on this whole affair. He said no. He got somebody to type up what was on the tapes and he left off the stuff that was embarrassing. Still the judge asked him to hand over all the tapes. He still said no. Finally he handed them over—but there was an eighteen-minute erased spot right in—you guessed it—an embarrassing part of the tape that would make him look guilty. But make no mistake, there was plenty of stuff that DID make him look right guilty, including proof that he knew all about the Watergate break-in as early as six days after it happened.

Let me make this point here: Nixon himself probably didn't EXACTLY know that the burglars were EXACTLY breaking into EXACTLY that office of democratic bigwigs. But he hired some guys and told them to do whatever it took to get him reelected. They chose to do stuff like breakin' in and bugging. And when they told the president, he didn't say "Stop it! I didn't mean anything ILLEGAL!" No sir, he just set about trying to cover the whole thing up.

Not a good deal.

So it was in . . . let me see, I think I have it written down . . . in the springtime of 1974 when we began to hear that word "impeach" that we had never heard before. What it exactly meant was to bring criminal charges against the president and have a trial in the Senate. Everybody was real chicken about doing this, even though the evidence looked quite bad against old Nixon. In the end, though, this tough decision didn't have to be made because the president stepped down. On, let's see, August 8, 1974, *(consulting notebook)* President Richard Nixon gave a speech to the nation, in which he said, "I shall resign the presidency effective at noon tomorrow." And he did.

I would like to say that it was a sad day, but the truth is, the whole affair had been so sad that we were relieved to have it over with. But it was sad, of course, that a person we trusted so much could make such wrong decisions and go off on such a bad, illegal course, you know?

Goodnight nurse, how I do go on when I get wound up! I hope I haven't bored you silly with my memories. It was an interesting time in history—which I started, as I think I mentioned. And everything I told you is true, I promise.

I have it written down.

Love You Not Me?

A Lighthearted but Historical Duet for a Boy and a Girl

About Love You Not Me?

Perhaps you have read a book or seen a movie about Native American princess Pocahontas and her relationship with John Smith and the other settlers at Jamestown. The following duet acting scene attempts, in a lighthearted way, to dispel some of the myths surrounding this legendary young woman and her relationships. You may feel slightly different about how she and those around her have been portrayed after you have read and worked on this piece.

This is a scene which may be expanded to include others in your class if you wish. As Pocahontas and John Smith chat about events, it is possible to have other actors portray the scenes in another part of your acting area. Maybe you would even like to insert lines of dialogue for them, such as "Let's watch how it really happened!" or "Look over here, it's going on right before your eyes!"

Regardless of whether John Smith and Pocahontas were really romantically involved, were "like brother and sister," or whether John Smith used Pocahontas for personal gain, it is obvious that a strong bond existed between them. When portraying these two characters, it is important to show that affection and regard. Their banter is punctuated by occasional poignant pauses, times when they are forced to reflect on their time together.

Though we use the phrase "Native American" to refer to those original Americans today, the use of the term "Indian" in this scene is meant to call to mind the terminology of the day. Feel free to change it if you like.

This is a scene in which some period costuming would most likely enhance the presentation for your audience. Visit your library for books on the clothing of the day, especially for John Smith. You might want to experiment with a beard for him—it was fairly astonishing to the native Americans that these Englishmen all had beards. One even shot an arrow through a beard once. You can purchase "crepe hair" in a braid at a costume or magic store and attach it to your actor's face with a glue that is made especially for faces called "spirit gum." Or you can surely acquire a ready-made beard at the same store. As for Pocahontas, she was an Algonquin Indian. It should be fairly easy and interesting to research the clothing of these people—they wore hairstyles to indicate whether they were married or single, etc. A book entitled *The Algonquins* by N.C. Murfreesboro, published by Johnson Publishing Co., 1972, may help you with a description.

Exercises to Accompany *Love You Not Me?*

1. Do you think it's proper for Hollywood to take a figure such as Pocahontas, who really lived, and create a fictitious motion picture about her life, creating characters and events that probably didn't happen—or changing the events that did happen in such a way as to make them more interesting or romantic? Discuss what is meant by "artistic license" and give your opinions about it. Is it a way for many people to know about a legendary person in history—or is it exploitation? How would you feel if one of your ancestors was portrayed in a way that was not historically accurate?

2. At one point in the scene, Pocahontas states that she has been "let down" by more than one man in her life. Discuss how John Smith, Powhatan, John Rolfe, and Japizaw each disappointed Pocahontas and changed the course of her life.

3. As you begin work on this duet, you may wish to read more about the life of this legendary princess. If so, see if you can form a mental picture about the kind of girl and woman she was. Do you think she was friendly and amicable toward these new people? Did she really want to help them, or was she just obedient to her father? Did she have a strong will? Imagine yourself in her place. Would you be as open-minded and willing to help?

4. Here are some more materials about Pocahontas and her people.

The Virginia Colony by Dennis B. Fradin. Chicago: Children's Press, 1986.

The Double Life of Pocahontas by Jean Fritz. New York: Putman, 1983.

John Smith by Charles P. Graves. New York: Chelsea House, 1991.

Pocahontas: Powhatan Peacemaker by Anne Holler. New York: Chelsea House, 1993.

The Powhatan Indians by Melissa McDaniel. New York: Chelsea House, 1995.

Love You Not Me?

A Lighthearted yet Historical Duet for a Boy and a Girl

(The scene begins with John Smith on stage. He addresses the audience with a big smile.)

John Smith: Hello, everyone, John Smith here. Yes, THE John Smith, Pocahontas's best friend and, well, I don't want to brag, but I was sort of her boyfriend.

(Pocahontas enters and stands behind him.)

Pocahontas: What a liar and a scoundrel!

John: Pocahontas!

Pocahontas *(coming to the front of the stage)*: I'm sure I'm the last person you want to see as you spin your wild self-serving yarns.

John: No! I mean, I'm glad to see you! You're like a kid sister to me.

Pocahontas: A kid sister? Who are you trying to kid?

John: Now Pocahontas, this class has invited me to come and tell the story of me and you and Jamestown and Powhatan . . .

Pocahontas: This ought to be good . . .

John: Well, maybe you want to be on your way and let me tell it?

Pocahontas: Not a chance, buster. I'm going to stay right here and make sure you're . . . shall we say . . . historically accurate?

John *(nervously clearing throat)*: Well, okay . . . it all started in 1595 when you, Pocahontas, were born in what is now known as Virginia. How am I doing so far?

Pocahontas: Not too bad. It was beautiful country—wild, untamed land, rich with cherry trees and red ripe strawberries. My father was Powhatan, king of many Indian tribes. I was his very favorite daughter . . .

John: That may be true, but he sure had enough of them! Over 100 wives!

Pocahontas: He was a king! He had benefits!

John: He would marry a woman, have a child with her, then send her back to the village and get another. Sort of like "trading her in on a newer model."

Pocahontas: Are you quite finished?

John: No. In April of 1607, when we English arrived at Chesapeake Bay, there was a lot of responsibility on our shoulders. The English government was really jealous of Spain because of Christopher Columbus. What made it even worse was that he had come to England first and we turned him away! So we were supposed to find gold. We were supposed to find a shortcut to the other ocean. We were . . .

Pocahontas: You were supposed to convert all the Indians to Christianity.

John: Well . . . yes! What was so wrong with that?

Pocahontas: Maybe we were just fine as we were!

John: You were savages!

Pocahontas: We were not savages. We worshiped our god Okee who held all danger in his hands. Floods, sickness, war . . . Englishmen.

John: As I was saying . . . we built a fort and settled in. However, we couldn't help but notice natives sneaking up in the grass. We were so friendly! We clapped our hands over our hearts in the sign of friendship . . .

Pocahontas: And we responded the same way! We lowered our bows and even gave you gifts!

John: Yes you did. To be fair, you did give us corn in trade for some things . . . like beads . . .

Pocahontas: My father always wanted weapons, and you never gave him so much as a beebee gun!

John: What's a beebee gun?

Pocahontas: Oh never mind, not invented yet. My point is, my father trusted you! He took you into his tribe!

John: Because of you . . .

Pocahontas: Well, that's true, if I do say so myself. See, here's what happened. This is the real story of John Smith, great tough guy who had fought the Turks in Europe. He had all sorts of rugged experiences before coming to the New World. He'd been captured, he'd been made a slave. He felt as if he knew all about how to handle us "savages." So he's in this brave New World, right? "New" to him . . . we'd been here all along. Anyway, he's exploring. He's looking for gold, he's looking for that other ocean that just surely must be around the next bend . . . and he got . . .

John: I got ambushed by Pamnukey Indians! One of your dad's tribes!

Pocahontas: And what did you do? Indians circled all around you . . . and brave John Smith, had an Indian guide . . .

John: Yes I did, what of it?

Pocahontas: What of it? You put him in front of you and used him as a shield, that's what of it! You waved your big scary gun in the air and started backing up—but you fell . . . *(laughing)* you fell . . .

John: Just go ahead and say it! I fell into a swamp! The uncivilized land was full of traps like swamps.

Pocahontas: Indians had to pull your oozy self out of that swamp and they hauled you off to Powhatan, my father, the king.

John: I will confess he was a scary man to do business with. Seated up high on a throne—all decked out in robes and jewelry. And as if I wasn't scared enough, they called the priests—and laid me out as if they were going to make a sacrifice of me!

Pocahontas: And I came in and saved your worthless . . . self.

John: Yes, but I don't think you were just being nice.

Pocahontas: What do you mean?

John: I think it was just so your dad could "adopt" me into his tribe and make me his subject. I think it was all prearranged by the two of you.

Pocahontas: You mean you think that if an Indian princess throws herself over a man and saves his life then he is her brother and part of the tribe?

John: Yes!

Pocahontas: You think it was like an Indian ritual that we had done before?

John: I think chances are really good.

Pocahontas: Well, maybe that was it. Maybe I just liked you. Maybe I had just never seen anybody so ugly with so much hair on his face.

John: You befriended me, though.

Pocahontas: Yes, I did. I loved you like a brother. I felt that you were part of my world and I was part of yours. You taught me English, I taught you my native language.

John: You said some things that made us laugh.

Pocahontas: I know what you're going to say . . . "Love you not me."

John: Yes! What did you mean, girl?

Pocahontas *(somewhat sadly)*: I meant . . . "Do you love me?"

(a silence)

And you tricked my father! When I saved your life, you were part of his tribe from then on, and under his rule! He explained that to you and you acted as if you understood!

John: Of course I did! I was being held captive! I would've agreed that my mother was a wild boar to be allowed to escape! But I promised him presents, didn't I?

Pocahontas: Oh yes, tell them what you promised him.

John: He asked me for a millstone for grinding corn and a cannon.

Pocahontas: So you led twelve Indian guards back to Jamestown.

John: And said, "Here you go! Here's the cannon! Here's the millstone!"

Pocahontas: Yes, but the millstone could not be moved by all twelve men, and the cannon weighed in the neighborhood of 3500 pounds!

John: So? They should've picked lighter presents! I gave them bells, beads . . .

Pocahontas: Oh, John Smith.

John: Well, you have to admit, I was a good leader for Jamestown. I insisted that those lazy settlers work all day, planting crops and making homes.

Pocahontas: Yes, I admit you did make some improvements. And we Indians liked you! We felt we could trust you. We felt that you had joined us and had a foot in both worlds. Instead, one foot was on a banana peel . . .

John: Can I help it if some gunpowder exploded in my belt pouch?

Pocahontas: No. Well, yes. You could have taken your gunpowder pouch off and hung it up with your pants when you napped. But when you went back to England, to recover from your burns, they lied to us all! They told us you were dead!

John: But we met up again later! In London!

Pocahontas: Let me tell this in order! First, I was kidnapped. Princess-napped. I was tricked . . .

John: By some of your fellow Indians . . .

Pocahontas: There was an English ship in the harbor. Naturally I was curious about it. There was an Indian man named Japizaw and his wife. She said she wanted to go aboard the ship and look around. He said she needed another woman to go along. I finally agreed to go on board with her, though I knew my dad would never have approved. So I went. And the doors slammed and I was whisked off to Jamestown against my will. It had all been an act.

John: I never knew why they did that exactly.

Pocahontas: I was held captive so that my father would give up the guns he had stolen from the settlers and let some English captives go free. And agree to peace.

John: Surely he jumped to accept that offer! Guns . . . captives . . . a small price to pay for his daughter's safe return!

Pocahontas: No. Actually, I've been let down by more than one man in my life, John Smith. My father left me in Jamestown!

John: But it turned out okay. You turned to Christianity and accepted our God as yours . . .

Pocahontas: I was lonely, John Smith. I had always been around brothers and sisters . . .

John: With a hundred stepmoms, I guess so!

Pocahontas: And so I just started listening to this Reverend Whitaker who had been hired to convert me. I didn't exactly believe that my old ways were evil and wrong—but it seemed necessary to say so. So I did.

John: Then you met the other John in your life.

Pocahontas: John Rolfe.

John: Whom you married.

Pocahontas: Yes, I did. I loved John Rolfe. He was determined to raise tobacco which I thought was stinky and smelly, but I loved him. And when he asked my father for my hand in marriage, I think my father viewed it as a way to set me free without actually giving in and handing over guns and prisoners. If we were suddenly all on the same side, he didn't have to surrender, you see?

John: So he said yes?

Pocahontas: He not only said yes, he sent a string of pearls as a wedding present.

John: Something old? Something blue?

Pocahontas: What?

John: Never mind.

Pocahontas: I have to admit that I took some pleasure in sending word to my father that I was going to marry an Englishman and thereby become English and he could put that in his pipe and smoke it!

John: So how did you end up in England? Where we met again.

Pocahontas: At the time I didn't quite understand, but I think it was all a big publicity stunt, you know? Like a good ad campaign? The folks in London who had all the money didn't think things were going so well in the New World. They had sent supplies and additional settlers, and yet nobody in the New World was finding any gold or making any tar or harvesting any pineapples—the only thing they were good at, it seemed, was converting savages.

John: So if you showed up and acted all converted and civilized . . .

Pocahontas: More money would flow from the Virginia Company of London. But I didn't know any of that at the time. By then I had a wonderful little son named Thomas and I thought it would be interesting for us both to see the great city of London. My father sent a special ambassador with me—Tomocomo was his name—and asked Tomocomo to tell him all about London. He wanted a head count of how many people lived there. He gave Tomocomo a stick and told him to make notches for every person he saw.

John: I bet Tomocomo threw that stick away the minute he got off the ship!

Pocahontas: No kidding! London was horrible, John Smith. Giant and crowded and dirty and everything for sale, for sale at the top of people's lungs, yelling out in the street. We stayed there as long as we could stand it, and were treated rather grandly, I must confess. I didn't care for the stiff dresses with lace and tight leather shoes they asked me to wear, but I was very happy to be in London . . . where, I now knew, a certain friend of mine lived.

John: Do you mean me?

Pocahontas: Of course I do, who else? I waited for you to call on me! I believed you would come because now we were countrymen! You had called Powhatan "father," which meant that you were one of us! But you never came.

John: I was afraid, Pocahontas. I was afraid that you thought I was . . . more to you than I was willing to be.

Pocahontas: Coward.

John: I had written a letter to Queen Anne on your behalf! I praised you, told her how you had helped the settlers at Jamestown!

Pocahontas: Who are you trying to kid, John Smith? You just wanted to remind the queen what a huge role you had in the settling of Jamestown.

John: Plus, you were married.

Pocahontas: What?

John: You were another man's wife! I thought it might be awkward.

Pocahontas: You finally showed up. After we had moved to the country for my health.

John: Yes, I called on you. And you covered your face with your hands and turned away.

Pocahontas: I was completely stunned to see you! I had no warning! I just went to the door and there stood my old friend, my "brother" John Smith! I was very upset.

John: Well, you soon let me know where you stood.

Pocahontas: I said, *"You did promise Powhatan what was yours should bee his, and the like to you; you called him father, being in his land a stranger, and by the same reason so must I doe you."* I scolded you for letting them tell me you were dead. I said that forever more from that day we would be countrymen. But I never saw you again.

(another silence)

John: In my own way, Pocahontas, I did love you like a sister. You showed me kindness in a world full of fear and savagery. You turned cartwheels in the streets of my city and strung beads with the children of my friends.

Pocahontas: And I can't say that you didn't enrich my life, John Smith. Through you I learned of another entire race of people, of a life I never would have touched otherwise. The lines of our lives intersected, and we were both changed . . . and I think better for it.

John: Love you not me, Pocahontas?

Pocahontas: I do, John Smith. Always. *(a brief pause)* Is this where we sing about the color of the wind?

John: I don't think so. God be with you, Pocahontas.

Pocahontas: And may Okee be with you, John Smith.

Pocahontas and John Smith: And with all of you.

Cinderella!

A Full-Length Play to Perform for Children

About Cinderella!

Cinderella!? Please, a fairy tale! What are we, thumbsuckers?

Not at all, and that's just the point. It's wonderful fun to perform children's theatre—that is, theatre for an audience of youngsters, presented by older students of drama. It's an opportunity for you to help introduce elementary-age kids to a world you've already begun to enjoy—the world of performing arts. Could children from your district be bused to a performance during the holiday season or at the end of school as a special field trip? Or is there a group of youngsters with special needs in your area, such as an orphanage, or a school for the learning disabled? And P.S.—youngsters make the best audience in the world! They will believe you ARE "Cinderella" or "The Prince" or "Eartha Cat" . . . and will be standing in line after the performance for your autograph.

The following version of Cinderella is an original adaptation of the familiar fairy tale. That is, we have taken a story which already exists, and turned it into a play with dialogue and stage directions, and a few new characters. We have stayed true to the original story line, which is an important part of adaptation. But we have modernized the story a bit, added some humor, and made the fact that Cinderella is a good, nice, and well-intentioned person a little bit more important than the fact that she may be beautiful. Some playwrights adapt novels, biographies, even short stories. You have probably seen movies or television shows which were adapted from short novels that you enjoy reading. In those cases, permission was secured from the author of the original work.

In the case of Cinderella, however, we don't need to ask anyone's permission to use it because it is in the public domain. That means that it's been around for a long time. According to the United States Copyright Office, if a work has been in existence for at least seventy-five years, it may be adapted without permission of the original author. And I'm sure we can all agree that Cinderella is at least that old.

So have a terrific time being a famous star in front of the local elementary school—and ask your teacher to give you extra credit if you can find out why the cat's first name is "Eartha."

Adaptation Exercises to Accompany Cinderella!

Fairy Tales—but with a Twist

One of the good things about adapting an existing work is that you get to be excused from the responsibility of thinking up the story yourself! You know what happens and how it turns out. And you should stay true to those elements in a real adaptation. So you can use your imagination for different things—like a new slant on the story, or one or two unique characters who will delight your audiences even more.

Tell the story of "Goldilocks and the Three Bears," but in a different way. For instance, set the story in Japan. Goldilocks is "Black-PigTail-San," and she eats a bowl of rice instead of porridge. Or make the Three Bears a rock group camping out on the beach. Who is Goldilocks? Why does she happen upon them? What does she break in their tent? Or make the Bears members of a football team called "The Bears." Is Goldilocks necessarily a girl? Could he be a blond-haired quarterback from an opposing team, breaking into the Bears' hotel room at an out-of-town game? Don't worry about dialogue and scenes for this exercise—just use a couple of pages to retell the story with a different twist.

Adapting an Original Work

Create a scene from the following diary excerpt. Read it first and think about it for a few moments. How should it be set up? Should we see the main character writing in her diary and speaking aloud—and then walking to another part of the stage to act out the events that happened? If so, should she return to the diary at the end of the scene? Or should it just start at the point where she runs into Elizabeth? As in most adaptable pieces, some of the dialogue is given for you. You may use it as written, or rewrite it if you keep the same meaning. In this diary excerpt, however, it occasionally says something like "We started screaming at each other" but doesn't specifically say what was said. As the playwright, you'll need to "flesh out" the scene and give your characters words. When Jason says "Oh" and then leaves the girls, do you think he really says he has to wash an elephant, etc., or does the main character just think that's what he means? Think about the main character (you can give her a name, by the way!) and Elizabeth. What do they look like? Do they speak in any particular accent? It's not made clear in the excerpt, so you're free to be creative. How does the scene end? What's the last line and who says it? (You can add and subtract lines if you like, as long as the same ideas and events are conveyed.)

DEAR DIARY,

Today is the worst day of my life. I am going to record the events of the day so that, if I ever lose my mind and think that I have had a bad day, I will remember this day and it will seem good by comparison.

It all started when I got out of bed and noticed that I had a ZIT on my forehead. It was huge, the size of that giant Cyclops Greek monster thing that I heard of once, I don't remember where. And it could not be covered by makeup no matter how hard I tried. I couldn't make any part of my hair fall low enough to cover it. So I went to school looking like a ghoul from a horror movie, and here comes my friend Elizabeth. She tells me that she has heard from Marty Johnson's best friend Jason that Marty likes me. I am feeling dizzy from this when Jason starts to head our way. I turn my back to him so he won't see my zit; Elizabeth does the same. I yell at her, wondering why she is hiding. She starts yelling too and now we're yelling at each other and Jason interrupts us. He asks us what could possibly be wrong? We both stare at him as if

English were not our native tongue and I finally say, brilliantly, "We're talking about a movie we saw." Elizabeth kicks me. I kick her back. Jason asks me what movie . . . of course, because he can't imagine what movie would make us yell. Diary, believe me—I had a complete and utter brain shutdown. I stared at him. I stared at Elizabeth. I promise you that I couldn't think of any movie in the world. I was without any thought of any movie title. I just stared. It was like a bad dream where you want to run but you can't make your legs move. I wanted to answer, but I couldn't make my brain move. So I said, "Um . . . *Ben-Hur.*" Now, I want to make it clear that I have no idea what *Ben-Hur* is, or if it is even actually a movie. I just said the thing that came into my mind, finally, after many embarrassing seconds. He said, *"Ben-Hur?* What's it about?" I stared some more and looked at Elizabeth and looked at my shoes and looked at birds flying by. Finally I said, "Oh, you know. Stuff." He said, "Oh," and then added that he had to go to class, or go wash an elephant, or go repel down the side of a building, anything to get away. As he walked away, Elizabeth and I started to scream at each other again. And just as I thought things couldn't get any worse, my dreaded little brother Tim came up to me and said, "Say, what's that on your head? You know, they make all kinds of cosmetics now."

I'm miserable.

I'm ready to be asleep.

Adapting Something Really Unusual

As a classroom exercise, experiment with adapting something a little "different." Find some written work that interests you, that speaks to you in some way. It can be a tragic or funny current event from the newspaper or a newsmagazine. It can be a poem, or the lyrics to a popular song. (Since this is just for classroom use, rather than a public viewing where admission is charged, you can use almost anything.) Write a page or two of dialogue based on this piece of work.

For example: You find an article in the newspaper about a new drug that may cure cancer or AIDS. Write a scene between the researcher who has made this discovery and his wife, who is proud of him. But give them a "conflict," or something that is wrong. Is she afraid that he will be exposed to AIDS if he conducts further experiments? Does he spend all of his time in the laboratory and none with his children? OR, write the scene between the researcher and the patient who will now have hope. OR, write the scene between the research scientist and the government official who has come to tell him there is no more money for his work. How would the scientist appeal to the humanity of the government official? How would he plead his case? Let your imagination take you wherever it can.

Production Needs: Cinderella!

Sound Cues

If you have a way to tape record certain music and sounds (such as on a cassette player or "jambox"), it will enhance your production to do so. Here are some suggestions:

- "Fairy music" for when the Fairy Godmother casts her spell on the pumpkins and mice—find something mystical and magical
- Heralding trumpets for when Eartha says "Tally ho!" and they leave for the ball, and again when Cinderella enters the ball.
- Ballroom dancing music
- A clock striking twelve . . . for you-know-when
- Jubilant wedding bells
- Processional music

Props

- Broom and dustrags for Cinderella
- Invitation to the ball
- Personal props for the Stepsisters and friends, including jewelry, lipstick, gloves, purses
- Wand for Fairy Godmother
- A quirt (can be easily made by attaching some fringed leather or fabric to the end of a magician's wand or other stick)
- Pumpkin
- Rat case with four tails hanging out or four little stuffed white rats (can be made without too much trouble—use fake fur or flannel. Just make a little round ball and give it a tail and whiskers—your audience will fill in the blanks)
- A compact
- Flowers for Cinderella at the wedding

Costumes

Your costume plan is going to depend on your budget. If you can go to a costume store and rent crowns and robes and cat costumes, go for it! If not, you'll need to get creative. (Remember—your audience will give you lots of mental leeway—if you can just suggest a costume, they'll take it the rest of the way in their imagination.) Don't forget the local Goodwill or Salvation Army or consignment shops—or your parents' closets. (But ask them first . . .)

Cinderella: She needs, of course, a tattered, sooty skirt and blouse for most of her scenes. See if you can find a "peasant blouse" (one with a drawstring at the neck) and give her a dark colored skirt. The ball dress is going to be more challenging, and will probably have to be sewn by someone's nice mother, or secured at a local second-hand store. This one dress needs to be as close as you can get to the real thing. For the wedding, see if you can find some white shiny material and make a cape to drape over Cinderella's ballgown. Those pesky glass slippers are a challenge also. The best thing would be a pair of see-through vinyl slippers—they do actually exist. If you can't find those, get any pair of white heels or pumps and glue tiny sequins or rhinestones on them. They'll be shiny and beautiful and give the illusion of glass.

Eartha: Suggest a cat outfit with black tights and a leotard or long black top. Give Eartha a pair of black gloves and glue long fake fingernails to them for claws. Make ears out of a bandeau (hard plastic headband) with construction paper ears glued on, or pin construction paper ears into her hair. Using an eyebrow pencil, paint whiskers on her face and add a nose. To experiment with a tail, attach a black belt to her seat, or put a black belt around her waist and cover a bent-out-straight coat hanger with black fake fur or corduroy. She needs a fancy coat to accompany Cinderella to the ball—try to find a second-hand black jacket (perhaps a man's) and sew tux tails to the bottom. Try to find a top hat at a party supply store.

Stepmother, Grosselda, Nausealina, Rumorelda, and Gossipella: These ladies need to look bad, but as if they're trying to look good. Too much makeup, too many strings of pearls (especially when the girls are ready for the ball), skirts that don't quite match the tops, etc. The Stepmother might need some baby powder in her hair for a little age, and she doesn't need additional accessories since she's not going to the ball. Have fun with these gals, they can look really goofy.

Fairy Godmother: She should look airy and magical. You might dress her in white or silver leotards and tights, then layer filmy, gauzy fabric on top, maybe in many different colors such as silver, blue, and pink. Give her a wreath of flowers on her head, if you like, maybe with ribbons hanging down.

Coachmen: The Coachmen have until recently been mice, so you might want to leave some whiskers on their cheeks. Dress them in something uniform—white turtlenecks with white jeans or even blue or black jeans, white gloves maybe black top hats from the same party supply house where Eartha's top hat was secured. Do they still have tails attached to their pants? It might be wise to think in terms of costume items that can quickly be removed to allow them to turn into Gentlemen of the Kingdom once Cinderella has been delivered to the ball, especially if they're good dancers. They may be in demand.

Prince: If he can stand it, the actor who plays the Prince probably really should wear a pair of tights on his legs and a long tunic top. (Come on, they make some really thick ones . . .) Perhaps someone could make him a reversible cape—red or some regal color for the ball, and white on the other side for the wedding. He'll need a crown. Again, look at the party supply store or fashion one out of cardboard and aluminum foil or bend thick pipe cleaners into the right shape.

Queen: Here's another character who needs a long, stately dress and, if possible, a royal cape. Look at the bathrobes in Mom's closets—could any of them create the illusion? She'll need a crown too; see **Prince.**

Ladies and Gentlemen of the Kingdom: The men can wear turtlenecks and dark slacks—or better yet, make the Prince feel better about his costume and let them all wear long tops and tights or leggings! Ladies can wear long dresses and skirts (Goodwill, Salvation Army, older sister's prom dress, Aunt Jennifer's maid of honor dress, etc.). Make some pointy cone hats out of cardboard and attach a scarf to the point on some. It might be fun to make all the folks in the kingdom dress in shades of the same color to make Cinderella stand out more when she arrives.

Scenery

Do as much or as little as you are able. You basically have the house, outside the house in the garden, and the ball. In the house, you need pieces of furniture for Cinderella to dust, and a sofa for the girls to swoon onto and chase each other around on. It might be nice to give Eartha a rug on which to curl up. Bring this stuff from home, or push classroom chairs together to represent the sofa. Cover them with an afghan and it will work. If you have scene painters and/or parents willing to build flats, have them make one with a door in it, and a window to look through to see the Prince coming up the walk. In the garden, you may want tall potted plants to give the appearance of trees or bushes. You may want to make handfuls of shiny stars and hang them from the ceiling with thread. You may wish to borrow a "mirror ball" and hang it for the ballroom scene. Or you may want to do this play on a "cafetorium" stage where you have no scenery and just pantomime everything. Again, this is the beauty and charm of children's theatre. As wonderful as it is to have the entire castle built onstage, it's not necessary. The youngsters will fill in the details themselves. (If you have any doubt, ask them to draw a picture of the play after they go back to their schools, and see if some details aren't there in crayon that weren't actually onstage!)

Your biggest scenic challenge is the coach. If you can get a patio chair or some other lightweight chair, have a teacher or parent attach it to two long pieces of wood. (How you attach it is going to depend upon what kind of chair it is and how expendable. If you find a legless old dining room chair in somebody's trash or at a garage sale, just nail it together with a hammer. If it's plastic, maybe it gets glued.) Make everything light enough so that Cinderella can sit in the chair and the four coachmen can each take a corner and physically lift her up by the lengthy pieces of wood. That's your base—now create the illusion of the orange pumpkin around the chair. You can purchase some flexible tubing which can be bent in a round shape and attached to the wood or the chair. Cover it with orange fake fur, felt, or puffs of orange tissue. The skeletal shape of a pumpkin will enable the kids to see Cinderella inside. Then fashion a "crown" out of green felt or pipe cleaners and set it on top. It will be reminiscent of a stem, and yet will look royal. Then Eartha helps Cinderella in and the Coachmen lift her up and carry her offstage or up the aisle.

Cast

(in order of appearance)

Cinderella
Eartha Cat
Stepmother
Grosselda, Cinderella's Stepsister
Nausealina, her other Stepsister
Rumorelda, the Stepsisters' friend
Gossipella, the Stepsisters' other friend
Fairy Godmother
Four Coachmen
Prince
Queen
Ladies and Gentlemen of the Kingdom

Cinderella!

A Full-Length Children's Play

SCENE 1

Cinderella *(entering, and speaking to audience)*: Hello, boys and girls! My name is Cinderella. I guess you may be thinking that "Cinderella" is a pretty funny name—not your usual Heather or Debbie. But I do a lot of housework, you see, and I always seem to have a smudge . . . or two . . . or three! of dirt on my face, often cinders from the fire. So—Cinderella is my name. You may have heard my story told before, or seen it in a movie or on television. But today it will be acted out for you, just as it really happened! So, first things first. I live in a house, which is not very big . . . in a kingdom, which is not very big . . . with my stepmother . . .

Eartha *(popping out)*: Who IS very big!

Cinderella: Oh now, that isn't nice!

Eartha: Did you say "mice"? Where are they?

Cinderella: This is my only pet—and sometimes I think my only friend—Eartha. Eartha Cat!

Eartha: Meow! At your service!

Cinderella: You'll have to forgive Eartha. Sometimes she is a little . . . outspoken.

Eartha: I just tell the truth! Poor Cinderella here lives with her EVIL, WICKED stepmother, and her two EVIL, WICKED, UGLY Stepsisters, Grosselda and Nausealina!

Cinderella: They were very kind to take me in when my father died, Eartha.

Eartha: Well they're terrible to you now, if you ask me . . . or even if you don't . . . they should know! *(indicates audience)* Boys and girls, those three are horrible to poor Cinderella! They make her do all the cooking and cleaning, including the scary places like behind their beds—and behind the toilet! And they never give her anything decent to wear—nothing from ___________, ever! *(insert name of popular local clothing store)*

Cinderella: Now, Eartha, they aren't as mean and cruel as all that. They give me plenty to eat, and my own room in which to sleep.

Eartha: Big whoop! You deserve better than food to eat and a place to sleep. Cinderella just won't admit how awful they are because she's too good a person ever to get mad at them. She's the nicest person I know—and my best friend!

Cinderella: Now come on, we've spent enough time talking. I have chores to do.

Eartha: Poor Cinderella. She always has chores to do. The only thing they don't make her do is . . . uh . . . *(polishing claws proudly)* catch the mice!

SCENE 2

(From offstage we hear, as Stepmother, Grosselda, and Nausealina enter . . .)

Stepmother: Cinderella! Cinderella! Where are you? One of the pins is coming out of my hair!

Cinderella *(enters, rushing, as Eartha comes along and stays close to Cinderella's heels)*: Here I am, ma'am. *(fixes pin)*

Stepmother: Where do you hide, girl? You're never around when I need you. And I always need you, this house is a mess!

Grosselda: She's always talking to that dopey cat, that's where!

(Eartha meows and spits in mad cat fashion.)

Nausealina: You'd better watch it, you bag of fleas, or you'll end up the fur trim on my coat!

(Eartha, temporarily subdued, curls up.)

Stepmother: There's so much dust around here I could write my name in it!

Eartha *(aside)*: If she knew how to spell her name.

Cinderella: I'm sorry, ma'am. I'll dust right away.

Grosselda: And Cinderella, what have you done with that petticoat I told you to wash? I need it right away!

Eartha *(aside)*: It's so huge, the Navy used it as a sail!

Cinderella: It's all ready, Grosselda. I'll get it for you.

Stepmother: Oh no, you don't! This floor needs sweeping. Quit wasting your time and get busy!

Cinderella: Yes, ma'am. *(scurries for broom)*

Grosselda: But Mother, I need that petticoat, I . . .

Nausealina: Oh, please let Cinderella get it for her so Grosselda'll quit wearing mine! She gets it all STINKY!

Grosselda: Stinky, huh? I'll make you think "stinky." *(They scuffle.)*

Stepmother: All right, you two. Stop your arguing. Cinderella, dust the furniture, sweep the floor, then get her petticoat.

Nausealina *(looking out window)*: Mother, mother, someone's coming up the walk!

Grosselda: Cinderella, don't just stand there, go open the door!

Stepmother: I swear I'll never get any work out of that girl.

Nausealina: It's Gossipella!

Grosselda: And Rumorelda!

Nausealina: They're holding something! What do they have?

Eartha: I don't know what they have but I'm about to have a stomachache! Ohh, those two! *(She rolls on her back, groaning.)*

(Enter Gossipella and Rumorelda.)

Rumorelda: Oh, this is just the end! Just a dream come true!

Gossipella: The chance of a lifetime! What every girl lives for!

Grosselda: Well—what is it?

Nausealina: Don't keep us guessing!

Eartha *(aside)*: Maybe they have train tickets out of town . . . ?

Rumorelda: But I'm speechless, I tell you! I don't think I can make my mouth form the words!

Gossipella: Me too! There's such a lump in my throat that I . . .

Stepmother: There will be such a lump on your head if you don't tell my girls this instant what it is that you're clutching!

Gossipella: Well, I don't know, Rumorelda, maybe we oughtn't tell them.

Rumorelda: They're sure to want to . . . GO!

Nausealina: Go? Go where?

Grosselda: You give me that paper! *(lunges for it)*

Gossipella: Oh, no you don't! *(running across the sofa)*

Grosselda: Give it here, Gossipella! *(running after her across the sofa)*

Rumorelda: Here, Gossipella! I'm clear, I'm clear!

Nausealina: Oh, no you're not! *(tackles her)*

Stepmother: You get off that sofa! Cinderella—footprints!

(Grosselda gets the letter . . . all four gather in front of sofa to read.)

Grosselda and Nausealina: "The Prince is giving a ball!"

(All four girls swoon onto the sofa.)

Grosselda and Nausealina *(sitting up)*: Who's invited?

Rumorelda and Gossipella *(sitting up also)*: All the single girls in the kingdom.

Grosselda, Nausealina, Rumorelda, and Gossipella: That's us!

(They swoon back, pause, think.)

When?

(All look at invitation.)

IN HALF AN HOUR!

(Pause, think, look down at clothes.)

WHAT WILL I WEAR?!

(Start to get up)

Rumorelda: Wait! There's a P.S.

Grosselda: "The Prince . . .

Nausealina: . . . wants . . .

Gossipella: . . . to pick . . .

Rumorelda: . . . a BRIDE . . ."

(All four freeze, staring with glazed expressions)

Stepmother *(behind them)*: THE PRINCE WANTS TO PICK A BRIDE?

Grosselda, Nausealina, Rumorelda, and Gossipella: That's me!

(All scatter as they try to get ready in a big hurry.)

Grosselda: Cinderella, where are my pearls?

Nausealina: A lipstick, Cinderella, I need a lipstick!

Rumorelda: Oh, Grosselda, could I please borrow some gloves? My hands sweat so, and . . .

Grosselda: I don't want your hands sweating in my gloves!

Nausealina: Cinderella, will you get over here and help me fix my hair?

Stepmother: Don't just stand around looking mooney, Cinderella, help the girls get ready! At last, a chance to get one of them married off!

Nausealina: Oh, what am I going to do? I would've had Cinderella make a new dress for me if I'd only known! Now I have to wear this old thing!

Gossipella: Don't worry! You look just fine in what you have on.

Nausealina: You're just lying so I'll look worse than you and you'll have a better chance with the Prince!

Rumorelda: Well, give that up, dearie—you three (Gossipella clears her throat) . . . oops, I mean you TWO don't have a chance!

Grosselda: Oh yeah?

Rumorelda: Yeah! *(They scuffle.)*

Stepmother: Will you stop arguing and get to that ball? Now, let me give you some tips. When you see the Prince, don't make bad jokes about him being a prince . . . got it? I mean, nothing like "beautiful place you have here . . . a regular 'palace'" or "my, but you entertain 'royally'" and especially not something like "I really am having a ball." Are you listening?

Grosselda, Nausealina, Rumorelda, and Gossipella: Yes, ma'am!

Stepmother: Good. Also remember that the way to a man's heart is through his ears and toes. So don't miss any opportunity to sing and dance for His Majesty. Singing and dancing are very important talents, and you must— *(sees that no one is listening)* Well, line up, let's have a look at you. *(The girls line up, are inspected one by one, and dash off.)* Good luck!

Rumorelda: Thanks! *(exits)*

Stepmother: Good luck!

Gossipella: Thanks! *(exits)*

Stepmother: Good luck!

Grosselda: Thanks! *(exits)*

Stepmother: Good luck!

Nausealina: Thanks! *(exits)*

(Eartha has gotten in line and waits for her hug.)

Stepmother: Cinderella, get this cat away from me!

Cinderella: Stepmother . . . I was wondering . . . perhaps . . . if I could have permission to . . . that is . . . I would like very much to be allowed to go to the ball.

Stepmother: You can't be serious! *(laughs rudely)* Girl, have you lost your mind? Do you think for one minute that I would allow someone of your lack of quality to be seen at the palace of the King? Someone covered in cinders from head to toe?

Cinderella: I would wash my face, Stepmother, and . . .

Stepmother: Cinderella, it is absolutely out of the question! What would the Prince want with the likes of you anyway? He surely has enough maids and servant girls! Now stop this foolish daydreaming and get to work. I'm going to go down to the castle and spy through the windows. When I return, I expect to see this place spotless! Cinderella . . . at the ball! The very idea! *(exits)*

SCENE 3

(Eartha and Cinderella are left behind. Eartha hisses after the Stepmother.)

Eartha: If she wasn't your stepmother, Cinderella, I swear I'd . . . I'd . . . give her fleas! Oops, what am I thinking? She probably has fleas already!

Cinderella: She is hard to understand at times, isn't she, Eartha? I just wanted to see the palace . . . from the inside . . . do you think all the girls of the kingdom are there, Eartha? All except me?

Eartha: Cinderella, I . . .

Cinderella: Oh, enough of this feeling sorry for myself. Let's go outside into the garden and get a little air.

Eartha: Good idea. This house does get a bit stuffy.

(They exit to the garden.)

Cinderella: It's a beautiful night, isn't it Eartha? Look at the stars!

Eartha: A star's mighty good company.

Cinderella: And you're mighty good company, Eartha. I don't know what I'd do without you!

Eartha: Cinderella, I feel just terrible that you aren't getting to go to that ball! It just isn't fair! You're not only sweeter and nicer than those Stepsisters, but you're also an awful lot prettier! Those two are as ugly as dogs—oops! I said my most hated word!

Cinderella: I'm sure they mean well . . .

Eartha: They don't mean well, they're just mean. And the next time I see them . . .

Cinderella: Eartha, what's that noise?

Eartha: Meow! *(hides behind Cinderella's skirt)*

(Enter Fairy Godmother.)

Cinderella: Who . . . who are you?

Fairy Godmother: Why, I'm your Fairy Godmother, Cinderella.

Cinderella: Gosh! I didn't even know I had one!

Fairy Godmother: Most people do—people who are good and kind, that is. Eartha, come out! I won't hurt you!

Eartha: Oh, well, I wasn't really scared, I just . . . uh . . . that is, I thought I saw a mouse run behind Cinderella's skirt. Yeah, that's it, a mouse.

Fairy Godmother: Well, if you're not afraid, maybe I could just wave my magic wand at you, and . . .

Eartha *(running behind Cinderella's skirt again)*: Meow!

(Cinderella and Fairy Godmother laugh.)

Cinderella: Now, come out, Eartha, there's nothing to be afraid of! If she's my fairy godmother, she surely won't hurt you!

Eartha: But I saw a movie about a godFATHER once, and he hurt a lot of people!

Fairy Godmother: He wasn't one of my kind. I'm only here to help. In fact, I'm here to send Cinderella to the Prince's ball!

Eartha: Yippee, Cinderella, I knew it!

Cinderella: To the ball, Fairy Godmother?

Fairy Godmother: Gracious yes, child, and you'd better hurry or you'll miss the whole thing!

Cinderella: But I have nothing to wear! I don't want to seem disrespectful by appearing before His Majesty in these old rags!

Fairy Godmother: Now what kind of fairy godmother would I be if I hadn't thought of that? Run up to your room, Cinderella, and see if there isn't something there that might do.

Cinderella: But Fairy Godmother, there are no clothes in my room at all! I have only this one dress.

Fairy Godmother: Run along and look anyway, Cinderella. I think you will be surprised.

Cinderella: Oh! *(She runs into the house.)*

Eartha: Gosh, Fairy Godmother, I'm sorry I hid from you. You really are a kind fairy godmother.

Fairy Godmother: I'm glad you trust me, Eartha. May I say that you seemed pretty nervous for a while there—as nervous as a cat?

Eartha: Aw, Fairy Godmother, you're teasing me!

Fairy Godmother: Yes, I suppose I am a little. But we only tease those about whom we care very much.

Eartha: I tease Cinderella sometimes—and I care about her!

Fairy Godmother: I know you do—and she's lucky to have such a fine cat as a friend.

Eartha: Aw, shucks, I'm not so much.

Fairy Godmother: Well, Cinderella and I happen to think that you are. And Eartha, you know that there are CAT fairy godmothers too!

Eartha: Do you think I might have one?

Fairy Godmother: I wouldn't be at all surprised!

Eartha: Me-ow! Let's see—the thing Cinderella wants most in the world is to go to the ball—and here you are, sending her to the ball. So . . . maybe my fairy godcat will give me the thing I want most in the world!

Fairy Godmother: And what is that?

Eartha: A date with Garfield!

(Cinderella enters, dressed for the ball.)

Cinderella: Oh, Fairy Godmother, it's . . . it's . . .

Eartha: Beautiful! You look beautiful!

Cinderella: Oh, I don't know how to thank you! What a lovely dress . . . and these slippers . . . they're made of the most delicate glass!

Fairy Godmother: Goodness, let's not waste time! We've many things yet to do. For one thing, you'll need a coach.

Eartha: Like a football coach?

Fairy Godmother: No, my dear, a coach in which to ride! You can't just walk to the ball! Eartha, I hear you're a pretty fair rat catcher!

Eartha: The best there is!

Fairy Godmother: Then how about rounding up four healthy white rats for us!

Eartha: May I catch five—and keep one for a tip?

Fairy Godmother: Indeed you may. Oh, and a pumpkin too, please?

Eartha *(saluting)*: I'm on it!

(Exits.)

Cinderella: Am I really going to the ball? It seems too wonderful to be true!

Fairy Godmother: Yes, you are, my dear. You get to go to the ball like everyone else because you're good and kind and unselfish. The Prince will be the luckiest man in the world if he even gets to have a short chat with you. If he gets to dance with you, he'll be wondering where his Fairy Godmother is! But remember this, Cinderella. It is very important that you be at home by the stroke of midnight. For that is when all the magic wears off.

Cinderella: The magic?

Fairy Godmother: At least tonight's magic. You will remember, Cinderella?

Cinderella: Oh yes, Fairy Godmother. I will remember.

(Eartha enters, carrying mice and pumpkins.)

Eartha: Will these do?

Fairy Godmother: They will do nicely! Now, run and put them beside that tree.

(Points offstage.)

Eartha *(exiting with mice and pumpkin)*: Me-ow!

Fairy Godmother *(waving wand, as magic music plays)*:

Spirits of good, powers of right
Come to me this starry night.
A magic deed, I need to do
And elves and sprites, I call on you!
Pumpkin orange, rats of white
Grow and change for me tonight.
Pumpkin big and coachmen tall
Take Cinderella to the Prince's ball!

(Enter Coach and Coachmen followed by Eartha who has added a tuxedo coat or top hat and quirt.)

Cinderella: Oh!

Eartha: Look what she did! Look what she did!

Cinderella: Eartha Cat, what do you have on?

Eartha: I suppose I'm your coachman, er . . . coachperson . . . er . . . coachcat?

Cinderella: Oh, Fairy Godmother! *(hugs her)* It's all so beautiful! How can I thank you?

Fairy Godmother: By always staying as goodhearted as you are, no matter what! Now, get in, dear, and hurry! The Prince is waiting!

(Cinderella enters the coach and exits, calling.)

Cinderella: Good-bye, Fairy Godmother! And thank you!

Fairy Godmother: Remember, Cinderella—the stroke of midnight!

Cinderella: Oh yes, I will remember! Eartha?

Eartha: Tally ho!

(Heralding trumpet music plays.)

SCENE 4

(The ballroom of the palace. Ballroom dance music is heard. There is a short choreographed dance, the dance ends, the dancers clap softly and mingle about, talking softly with one another. Stepsisters enter.)

Grosselda: Well, where is that Prince? You'd think he'd show up at his own ball!

Nausealina: He's surely here someplace. This palace is so big, it's probably taking him all night to go from room to room!

Grosselda: This really is a beautiful palace. I'll make some changes, though, after we're married . . .

Nausealina: After you're married? You mean after he and I are wed. Once he hears me sing, he'll snap me up in a minute!

Grosselda: Once he hears you sing, he'll snap his lunch up in a minute! Wait until he gets to see me dance!

Nausealina: Forget it! Listen to this! *(She begins to sing horribly.)*

Grosselda: Stop! Stop! You're hurting my ears and dogs are starting to howl! Watch this! *(She starts to "dance.")*

Nausealina: You call that dancing? You look as if you're trying to stomp out a match!

Grosselda: Well, your singing sounds as if you're being burned with a match!

(The Prince enters and begins to talk to various couples. Girls are flirting and swooning.)

Grosselda: Oh! He's coming! The Prince is coming!

Nausealina: Where? Where?

Grosselda: No! Don't turn around! Get out your mirror!

Nausealina *(gets compact out of purse and uses it to look over her shoulder at the Prince)*: Have you ever seen anybody so good-looking in your life?

Grosselda *(thinks for a minute)*: Maybe _________ in ___________. *(Insert name of current good-looking actor and a current movie or TV show in which he can be seen.)*

(The girls consider for a moment, then . . .)

Nausealina and Grosselda: Naaah!

Nausealina: Oh no, he's coming this way!

Grosselda: Put away that compact!

Nausealina: How do I look?

Grosselda: Awful. How do I look?

Nausealina: Worse. *(starts to "sing")*

(Grosselda starts to "dance.")

Prince: Are you two ladies all right?

Nausealina: Oh yes, Your Majesty. I was just practicing my singing.

Prince: With a voice like yours, my dear, you could use the practice. To keep it sounding lovely, I mean . . .

Grosselda: Your Majesty, I was wondering if you noticed my dancing just now?

Prince: Oh yes, and I must tell you that it reminded me of someone very near and dear to me. Someone very special.

Grosselda: An old girlfriend, perhaps? An old flame?

Prince: My horse.

Grosselda: Oh.

Nausealina: Nice place you've got here, Your Majesty, a regular palace . . .

Prince: If you ladies will excuse me, I . . .

Nausealina: Oh, but wait, Your Majesty, I was just about to sing an all-time favorite—"Feelings"!

Grosselda: Let's just have one dance together . . .

Nausealina: We really are having a ball . . .

(The Queen enters and interrupts them.)

Queen: If you ladies do not mind, I must have a word with my son.

Nausealina: No indeed, Your Highness. We were through with our conversation.

Prince: Indeed, Mother, this conversation has been over for quite some time.

Grosselda: I really think mothers-in-law get too much bad publicity!

Queen: Son, I must tell you that . . . *(sees that the Stepsisters are eavesdropping)* Ladies, there are refreshments in the next room.

Nausealina: Thanks! We're not too hungry.

Queen: Why not just go taste some punch, anyway, hmmm? It's an old family recipe.

Nausealina: Probably lime sherbet.

Grosselda: Oh, I get it! You want to be alone with the Prince to . . . er . . . talk things over!

Nausealina: Like weddings, and BRIDES, and registering for china . . .

Queen: What clever young ladies! Now, if you'll excuse us?

(Nausealina and Grosselda exit, looking at each other and the audience knowingly, confident that the Queen must have her eye on one of them for the Prince.)

Queen: Now, son, I must tell you of the beautiful girl who just arrived! She was in the most extraordinary coach, and . . .

Prince: Oh, Mother, I'm so tired of meeting "beautiful girls"! Each one means well, but I feel . . . I don't know . . . like a judge at cheerleader tryouts!

Queen: But dear, this one really is lovely. And so dear. We spoke briefly, but I was completely charmed.

Prince: They're all "really lovely" and completely charming, Mother.

Queen *(looking after the Stepsisters)*: All of them, son?

Prince: Well . . . many of them.

Queen: I think you'll find this one to be different.

Prince: How could she be different? I'm sure she's just . . .

(Cinderella enters. The crowd parts and gradually exits. The Prince and Cinderella meet at center stage and dance a waltz to music that isn't really there. They stop and look into each other's eyes.)

Cinderella: Thank you so much, Your Majesty.

Prince: The pleasure was all mine. *(bows)*

Cinderella: It was very strange . . . we were dancing . . . and yet I heard no music.

Prince: I heard very beautiful music.

Cinderella: Did you?

Prince: But I must confess that it may have been in my heart.

Cinderella *(looks at him for a moment, not believing her ears, then turning away)*: Now I will leave you and you may dance with someone else.

Prince: Wait—don't go. Who are you?

Cinderella: Sir, forgive me, but I cannot tell you.

Prince: Then I will imagine your name for myself. Are you of royalty?

Cinderella *(laughing)*: Hardly, Your Majesty.

Prince: Do you live in this kingdom?

Cinderella: I do, yes.

Prince: Then why have I never seen you before tonight?

Cinderella: Your Majesty, I . . .

Prince: I know, you may not answer. So, I will ask you nothing more about yourself. It is enough for me to know that you are here, even if . . . "magic" is responsible.

Cinderella: You are not far from the truth, good sir.

Prince: It doesn't matter. What does matter is that the minute I saw you, I knew that you were the kindest, warmest person I would ever know. In your eyes, I see one who is unselfish and loving . . . as well as very, very beautiful.

Cinderella: Oh, sir, you speak so kindly—I do not know what to say!

Prince: Then say nothing—but give me your hand.

(He kisses it, as a clock begins to chime midnight.)

Cinderella: Your Majesty! What time do those bells chime?

Prince: Midnight, I think, but why . . .

Cinderella: Then I must go!

Prince: But wait!

Cinderella: I cannot wait an instant!

Prince: Please, what is your name? Come back!

(Cinderella exits, dropping her shoe accidentally as she runs. The Prince picks it up and looks at it as the Queen enters.)

Queen: Son! Here you are! I've looked everywhere for you! The guests are leaving and they want to say good-bye. *(notices that his mind is elsewhere)* There were a great many beautiful young ladies in the palace this evening, weren't there, son? And a few that were perhaps not beautiful as we usually think of it, but interesting . . . ah, my son. Something or someone is on your mind, I can tell.

Prince: Yes, good Mother, I've met . . .

Queen: I believe I know whom you've met. About this tall, was she not?

Prince: Indeed. And about this beautiful, and about this kind *(he is using his arms to show huge amounts)* and I've never known anyone like her!

Queen: Son, a very wise man once told me that when you meet someone who causes you to say, "I've never known anyone like that person," then you should marry that person.

Prince: Who was that very wise man?

Queen: Your father, the king. And I married him.

Prince *(hugs her)*: I must find her, Mother!

Queen: Well, what is her name?

Prince: That's just it—she wouldn't tell me! But when she ran, she lost this glass slipper. And I intend to try it on every girl in the kingdom until I find its owner!

Queen: Son, it's late! People will be sleeping. Wait until tomorrow.

Prince: I wouldn't be able to get any rest at all tonight. I'd rather spend the whole night and all of tomorrow knocking on doors!

Queen: Forgive me, people of my kingdom, for what I am about to allow—but go on, my dear. And be very careful!

(The Prince runs.)

And son . . .

(He pauses.)

Perhaps your old mother is not quite as old as you thought, eh?

(He blows her a kiss and they both exit.)

SCENE 6

(Back at the house, Cinderella is sweeping or dusting. Eartha is curled up. Sisters and Stepmother are furious.)

Grosselda: Don't give up, Mother, maybe he'll call.

Nausealina: Maybe he'll call his horse!

Grosselda: Why, you . . . *(doubling up her fist)*

Stepmother: So let me get this straight. He spent the whole time at the ball with one girl, huh? So this one girl stole his heart, and it was love at first sight, huh? Well, who in the world could that one girl have been?

(Eartha signals "Shhhh" to audience.)

Nausealina: It's plain that the Prince appreciates neither true beauty nor true talent!

Stepmother: So it comes down to this, does it? I spend all my life giving you voice lessons, dancing lessons, cooking lessons, lessons in grace and charm. You meet the Prince . . . THE PRINCE . . . and he doesn't ask either one of you to marry him. He doesn't even ask either one of you for a date! Is this the thanks I get? And I was worried about how to console the one of you that didn't get picked! Who's going to console me, now that neither one of you has been picked?

(Eartha volunteers by putting a helpful arm around her shoulders.)

Stepmother: Cinderella! Get this cat away from me!

(Eartha skips off in glee and lies back down.)

Grosselda *(looking out of the window)*: Mother! Mother!

Stepmother *(joining her)*: What is it, child, what is it?

Nausealina: It's the Prince! *(getting out compact and looking over her shoulder out the window)*

(Cinderella pretends to busy herself with getting some imaginary speck of dirt out of the way.)

Stepmother: He sure looks awful—as if he's been out all night!

Grosselda: He's coming up the walk!

Nausealina: He's coming here!

Stepmother: Then you have another chance! Now, don't blow this one!

(Stepsisters stand at attention in a line, while Stepmother goes to the door.)

Your Majesty! How wonderful of you to call! What may my SINGLE, UNMARRIED daughters and I do for you this morning?

Prince *(entering)*: Just have your daughters take off their shoes, ma'am.

Stepmother: Take off their shoes? Stockings also?

Prince: Just the shoes, ma'am.

(Grosselda and Nausealina start to "sing" and "dance." Stepmother signals "cut!" to them. The Prince looks sick.)

Prince: Girls, please, take off your shoes. I want to find the person who fits this shoe . . . and marry her.

(Nausealina and Grosselda swoon onto the sofa.)

Prince *(to Grosselda)*: We'll start with you.

Grosselda: Well, Sir, my feet are somewhat swollen from all the dancing I did last night at your most enjoyable ball.

Prince: Oh yes . . . now I remember you.

Grosselda: But I'm sure I can just . . . slip . . . it . . . on . . . *(strains and strains and finally gives up)*

Prince: I don't think the shoe is hers. Next?

Nausealina *(pointing toe in an obnoxious manner)*: Let me try my hand . . . er, foot . . . that is . . . hee hee hee . . .

(strains, also unsuccessfully)

Prince *(visibly relieved)*: Well, I guess that's that . . .

Stepmother: Er . . . Your Majesty . . . I just thought that I might try.

Prince *(aside)*: I can see that it's going to be one of those days . . .

Stepmother: I mean, I always say, if the shoe fits, wear it! Heh, heh. *(strains, trying to slip on the shoe)* Just a minute, let me air out my foot! It's a bit moist! *(She waves her foot around, Prince produces a handkerchief and breathes through it.)* There now.

(tries again)

Prince: Madam, I don't believe the lady for whom I search is here. Now, if you'll excuse me, I have many house calls to make.

(Eartha has been pushing Cinderella while the Stepmother tried on the shoe, and now she pushes her right into the Prince. Their eyes meet. The Prince looks at her and shows recognition.)

Prince: Miss, why did you not ask to try on the slipper?

Cinderella: Sir, forgive me—I cannot tell you.

Prince: Then I will ask you only one question. Will you try it on?

(He kneels and slips the slipper on Cinderella's foot. It fits!)

Eartha: Yippee! It fits! It fits!

Prince: Is it really you?

Cinderella: Yes, Your Majesty, it is I . . . and see? I have the other! *(producing the other shoe from her pocket)*

(Stepmother, Grosselda, and Nausealina screech and cover their mouths with eyes bugged out. Cinderella and the Prince kiss. Eartha covers her eyes.)

Eartha: Me-ow!

(They stop kissing and run off, followed by Eartha. The other three "come to" and start to ad lib lines such as, "But Your Majesty, there must be some mistake!" and flop on the sofa when it is obvious the Prince and Cinderella are not coming back. Gossipella and Rumorelda enter.)

Gossipella: Oh, I could just die!

Rumorelda: My life's ambition! Ruined!

Stepmother: Cinderella! Of all impossibilities!!

Nausealina: He just feels sorry for her, that's all.

Grosselda: How could he help but feel sorry for anyone that homely . . .

Rumorelda: That plain!

Gossipella: That . . . bogus! *(or other undesirable adjective of your cast's choice)*

Stepmother: She probably batted those baby blue eyes at him.

Nausealina: They're not really that blue . . . she must wear contacts!

Grosselda: Not to mention those fake eyelashes!

Stepmother: What I want to know is how he could stand to look at that dirty face for five minutes without throwing up!

Rumorelda: What I want to know is why he would want her and all her ugliness when he could have had one of us with all our beautifulness!

(They strike "beautiful" poses.)

Nausealina: She probably borrowed something of mine to wear to that ball!

Gossipella: She was melted and poured into that dress, wherever she got it!

Grosselda: The awful little wretch! I could claw her eyes out!

(Eartha enters, crosses in front of them, stops and says . . .)

Eartha: And they call ME a cat!

(The women raise hands to clobber her and chase her off stage as she says . . .)

Me-ow!

SCENE 7

(It's the wedding! The ballroom crowd is reassembled and wedding bells ding and dong. The crowd may do a little dance [if you need the time for the happy couple to change costumes], or go right to a "V" shape formation. Prince and Cinderella enter wearing crown and wedding attire. Cinderella has a bouquet. They walk to center to kiss. Eartha sneaks up from behind and pops her head between the couple. Laughing, they both kiss her on the cheek. Cinderella and the Prince start to exit. Cinderella pauses, turns, and tosses her bouquet to Eartha. Eartha is briefly stunned, then says . . .)

Eartha: Garfield, you're mine! I just love a happy ending! Good-bye, boys and girls!

(As processional music plays, dancers fill in the space left by Cinderella and the Prince at center stage and bow. They separate and run up the aisle and exit. Fairy Godmother and Queen enter and take their bows next, followed by Rumorelda and Gossipella, then Stepmother, then Eartha, then Cinderella and the Prince. Group bow, then split and exit up the aisle to a place where your young audience can meet the cast.)

CREATING BELIEVABLE CHARACTERS

When we play a person on stage, we need to know as much as we can about this person in order to make him or her "come alive" and seem real to our audience. This is much easier if we as actors know the character "inside out" before attempting to portray him or her.

Exercises

On the next page is a worksheet with many questions. Create a character and answer all of the questions about him or her. The first time through, invent a very normal, "everyday" sort of person, maybe based on someone you really know. You'll have to make up a good deal of the information, such as the character's past and facts about his parents. It doesn't matter if it's factual—this information is just for you as an actor. Then do the worksheet again, this time creating a completely wild and bizarre person. Even if the character is strange and exaggerated, it's possible to make him or her believable by knowing all there is to know about this person. Look at Jim Carey's character in *Ace Ventura, Pet Detective.* Could he be more "off the wall"? And yet we believe him because he acts as if he actually is that weird character. He has no doubt thoroughly researched the character.

Now pair off and create a scene in which one of your characters and the character of one of your classmates meet. Where are they? Why have they run into each other? What problem do they have and how do they solve it? How does the scene end? Improvise some dialogue at first (that is, make it up as you go along) and then go through it again, writing down the dialogue that you liked the most. The scene need not be lengthy—just two or three minutes.

The next time you are assigned a scene from an existing play, whether you're performing a monologue or a scene for two or more people, answer the questions on the Character Worksheet. Hang onto this worksheet—it can help you gain insight into any character you'll be playing.

Creating Believable Characters

Worksheet

1. What is the character's name? Is it an interesting name? Has the character gotten any special favors because of the name? Been treated badly because of it?
2. Where was the person born? Did he or she leave home quickly? When? Why?
3. Who are the character's parents? What kind of parents were they? Did they encourage your character? Belittle him or her? Have lots of laughter in their home, or run a "tight ship"?
4. What does your character believe in or care about?
5. How unusual or ordinary is your character? What do people notice about the character when he or she enters the room?
6. Is your character married, single, divorced, bold, shy, wild, funny, etc.?
7. What does your character enjoy doing? Does he or she have hobbies?
8. How does the character dress? Trendy? Casual? Hand-me-downs? What are his or her favorite colors? Does the character have some trademark item of clothing (such as a pin on the lapel or a backwards baseball cap)?
9. Is the character handsome, average, tall, short, fat? Athletic, gangly, clumsy?
10. What mannerisms does the character have? Hands move a lot? Fidgets? Always calm, no matter what is going on?
11. Is the character an achiever or "laid back"?
12. What things has the character saved from the past? What meanings do these things have?
13. What does the character think about society?
14. What are the character's goals? What does he or she dream about?
15. What is he or she scared of?